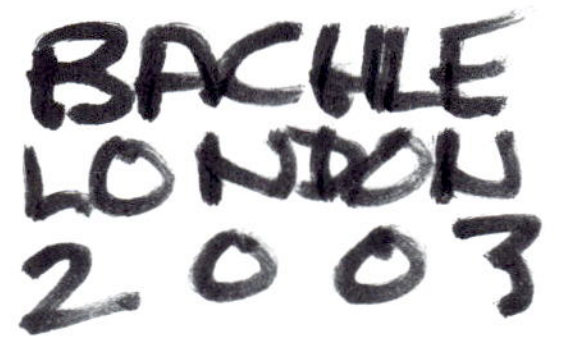

Corpus

Alejandra Figueroa

Corpus

Afterword by Philippe Sollers

with 69 tritone illustrations

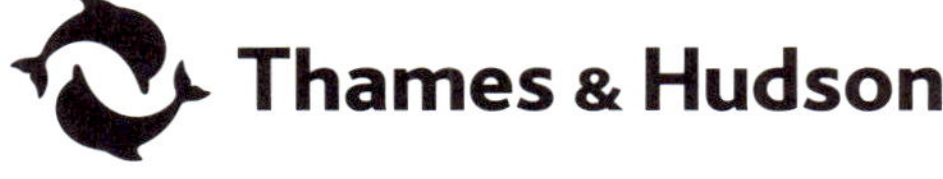

To my parents – I owe you more than my life.
To my precious friend – I owe you the inspiration and this book.

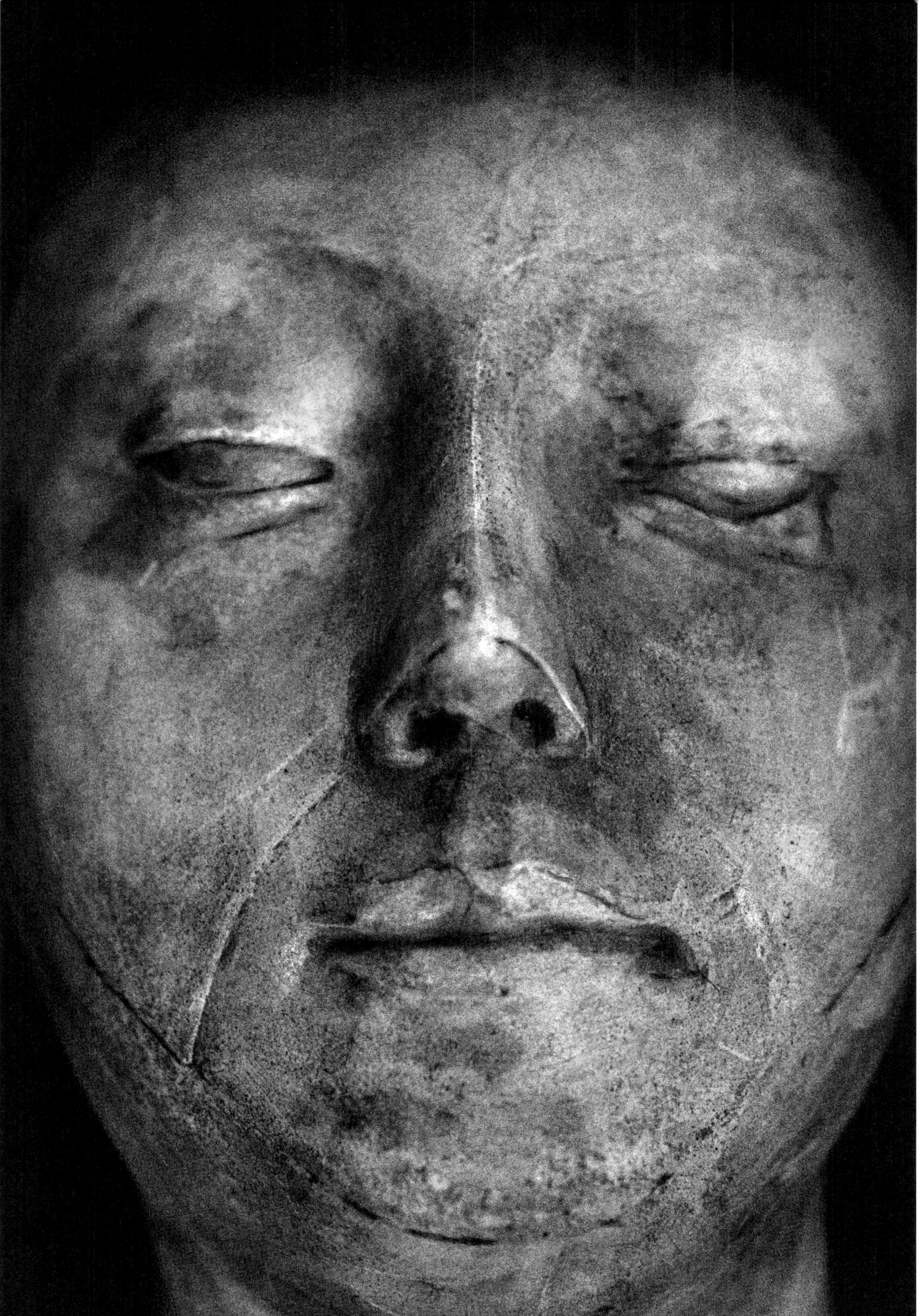

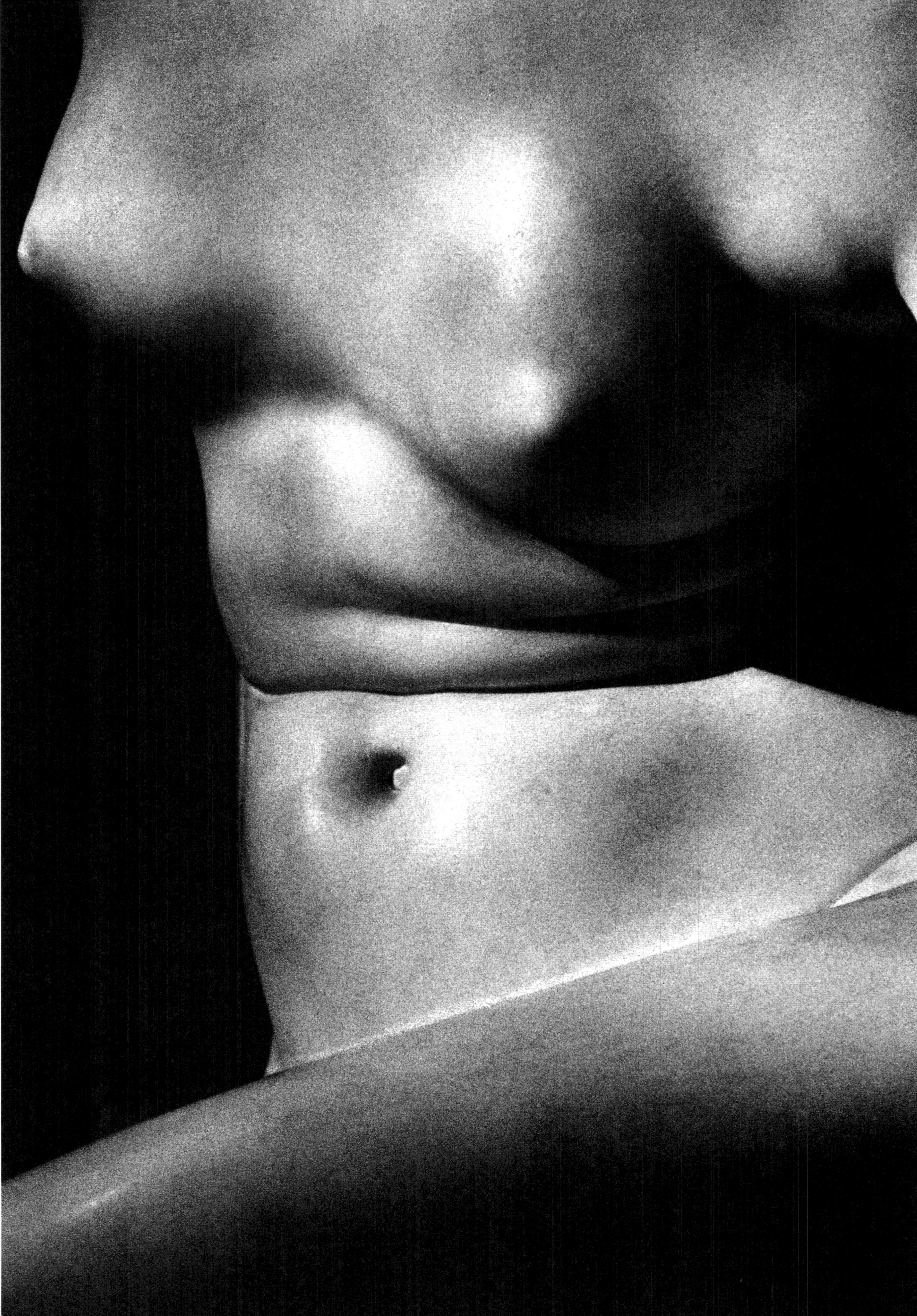

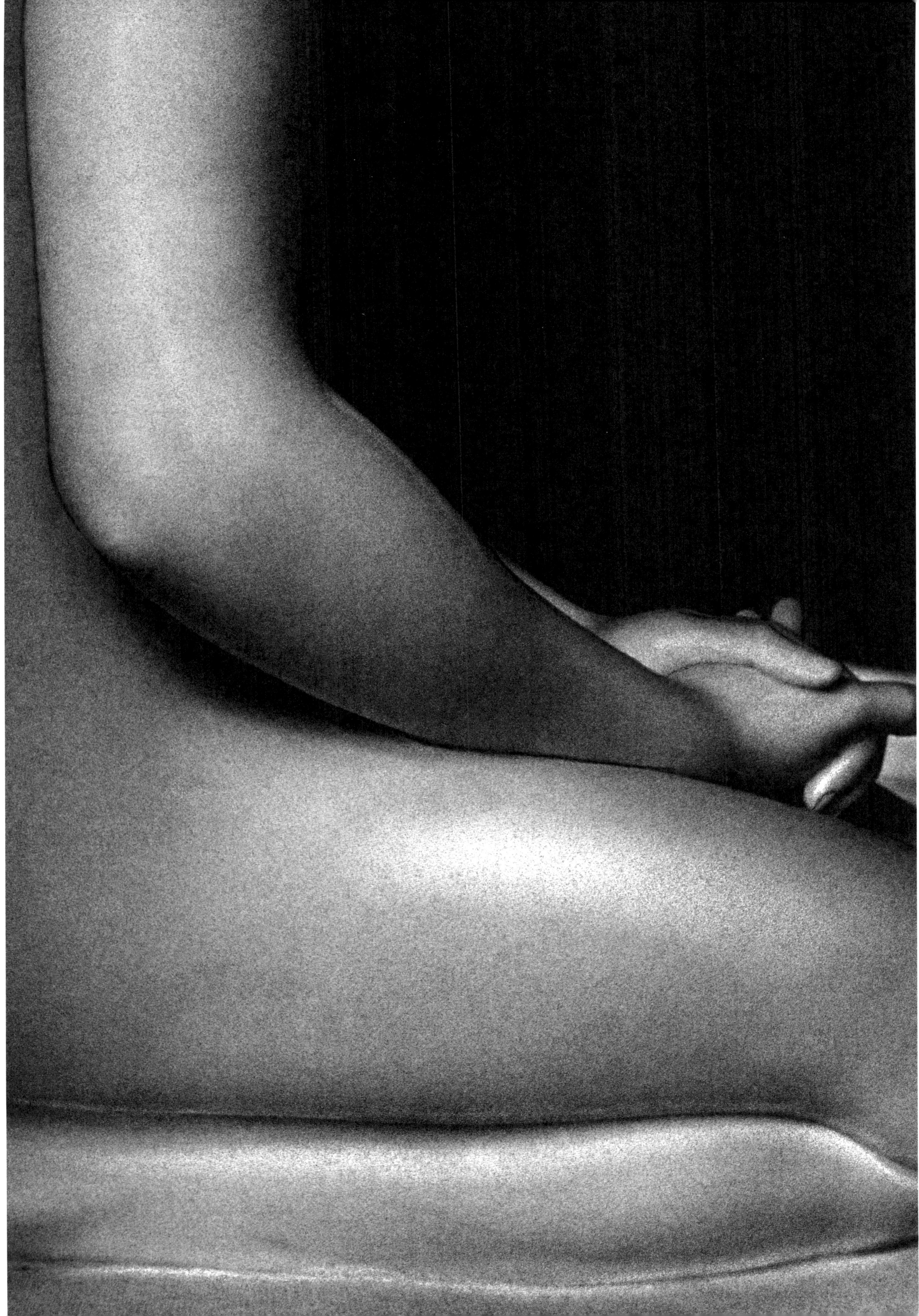

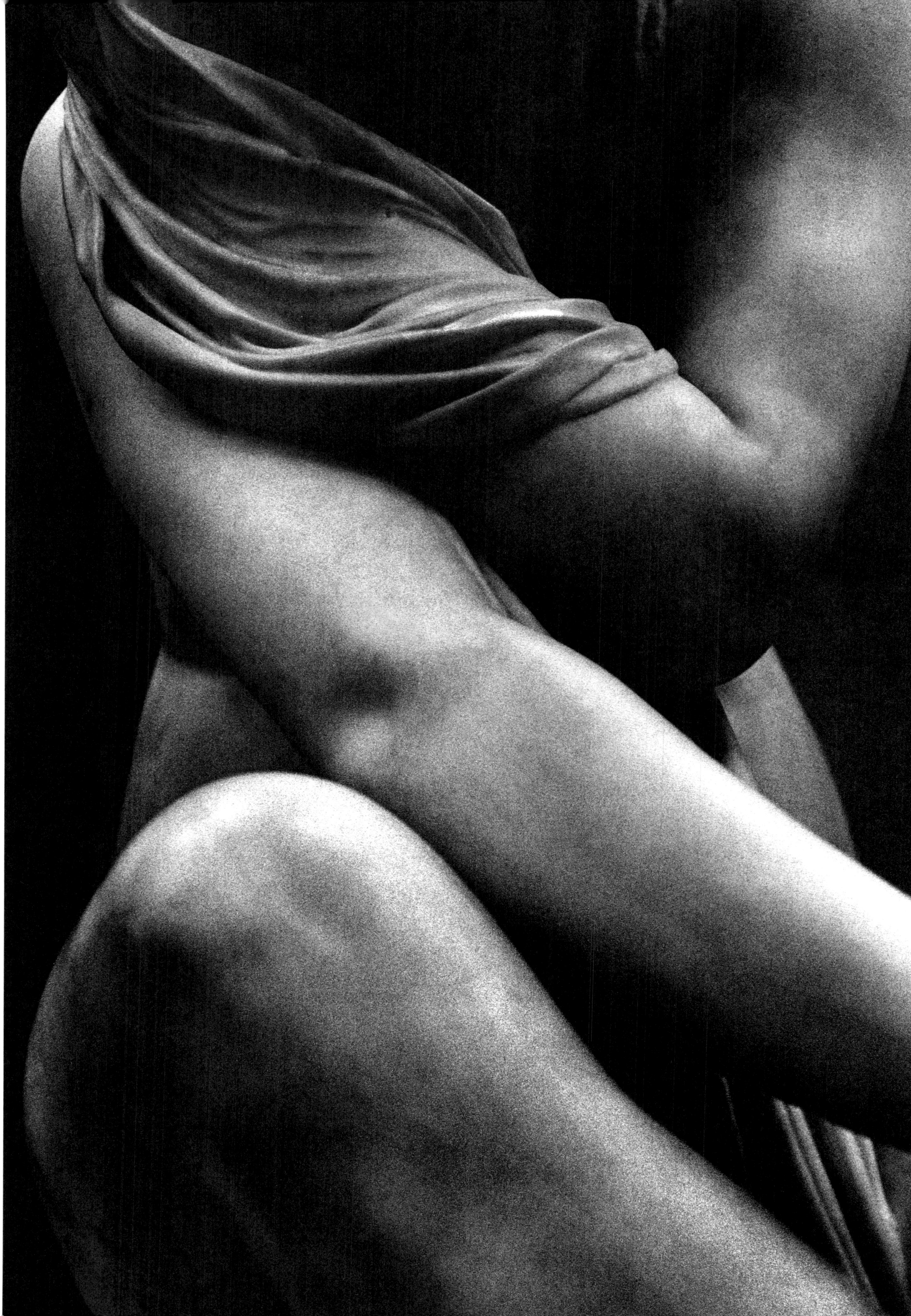

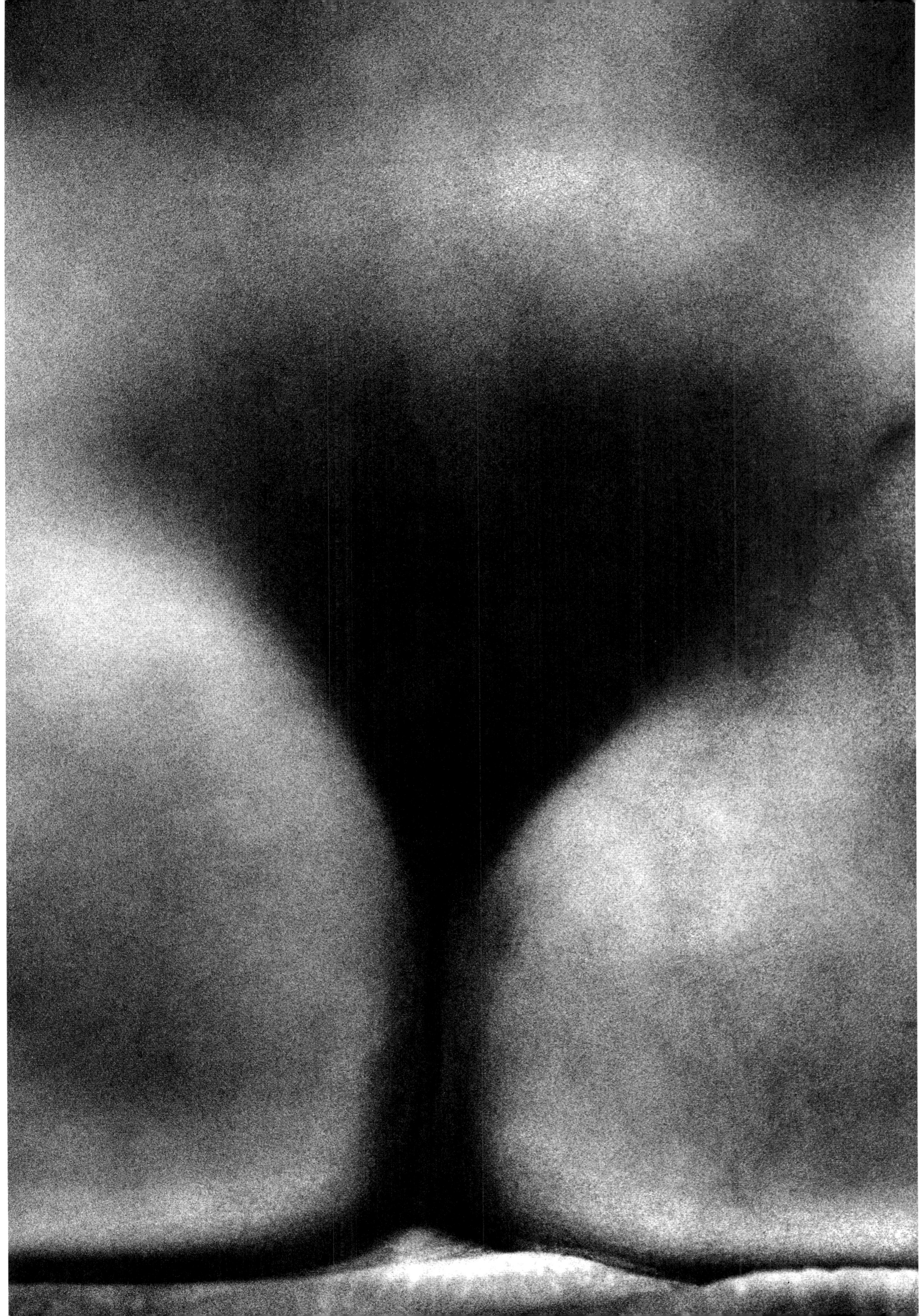

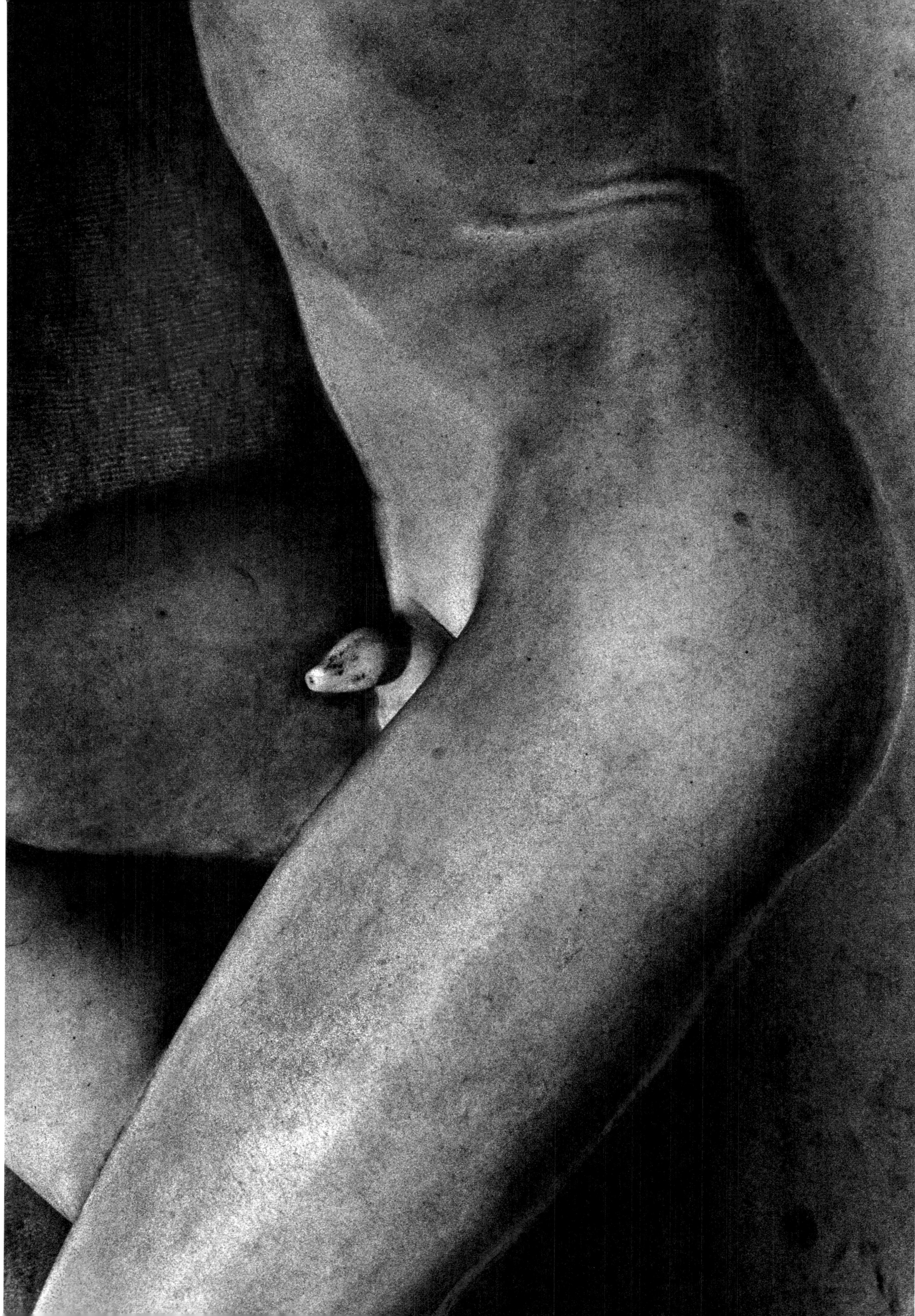

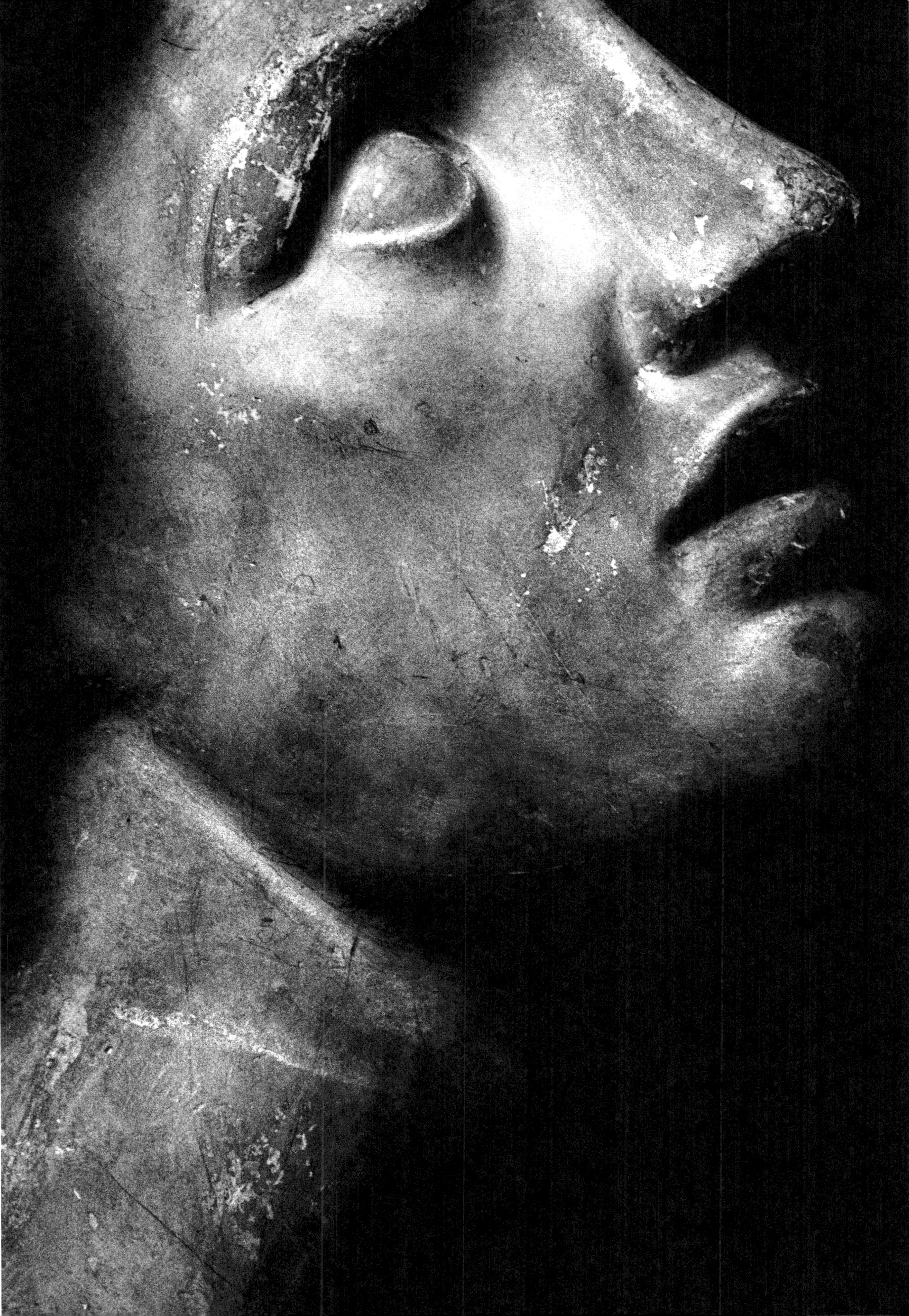

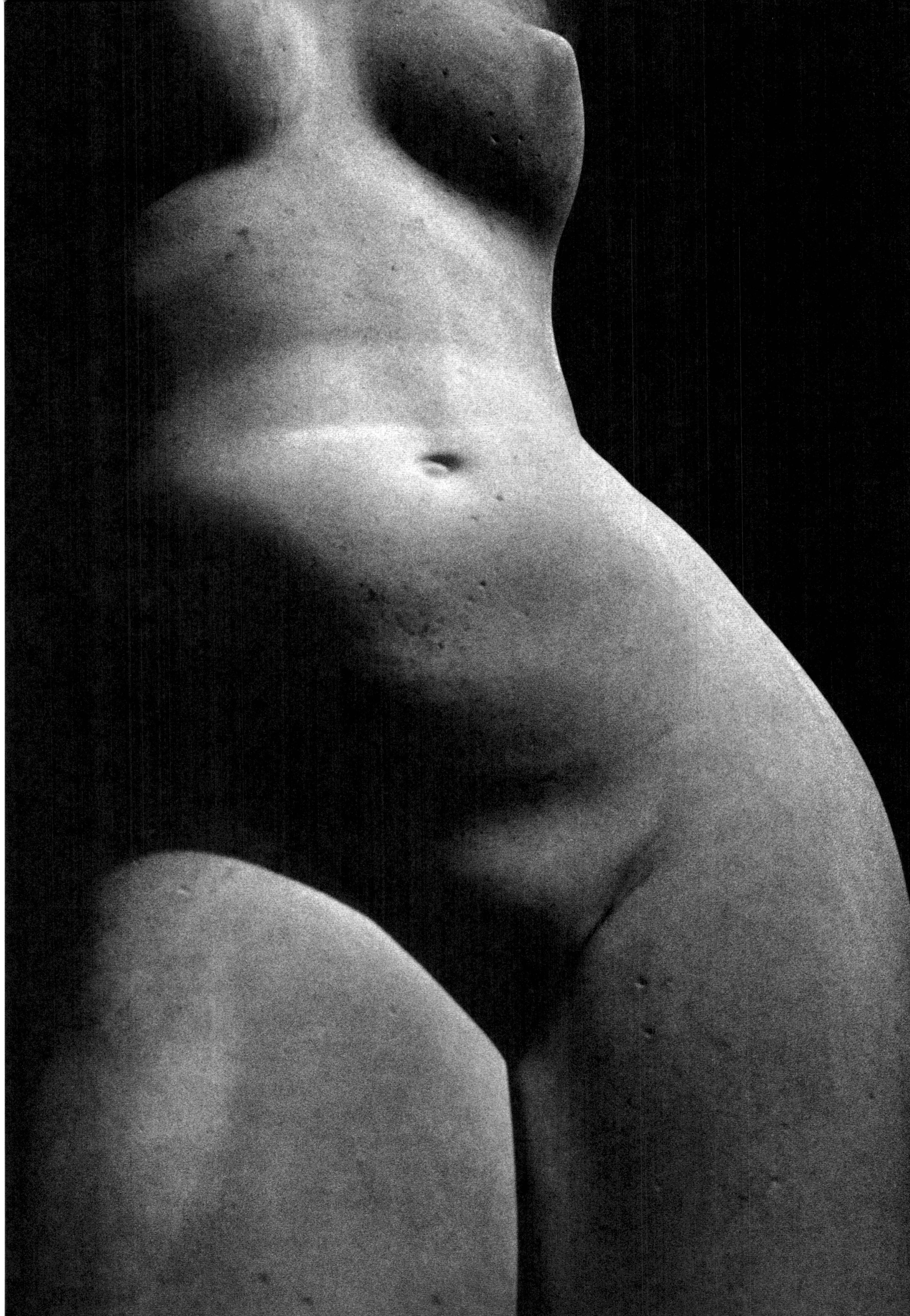

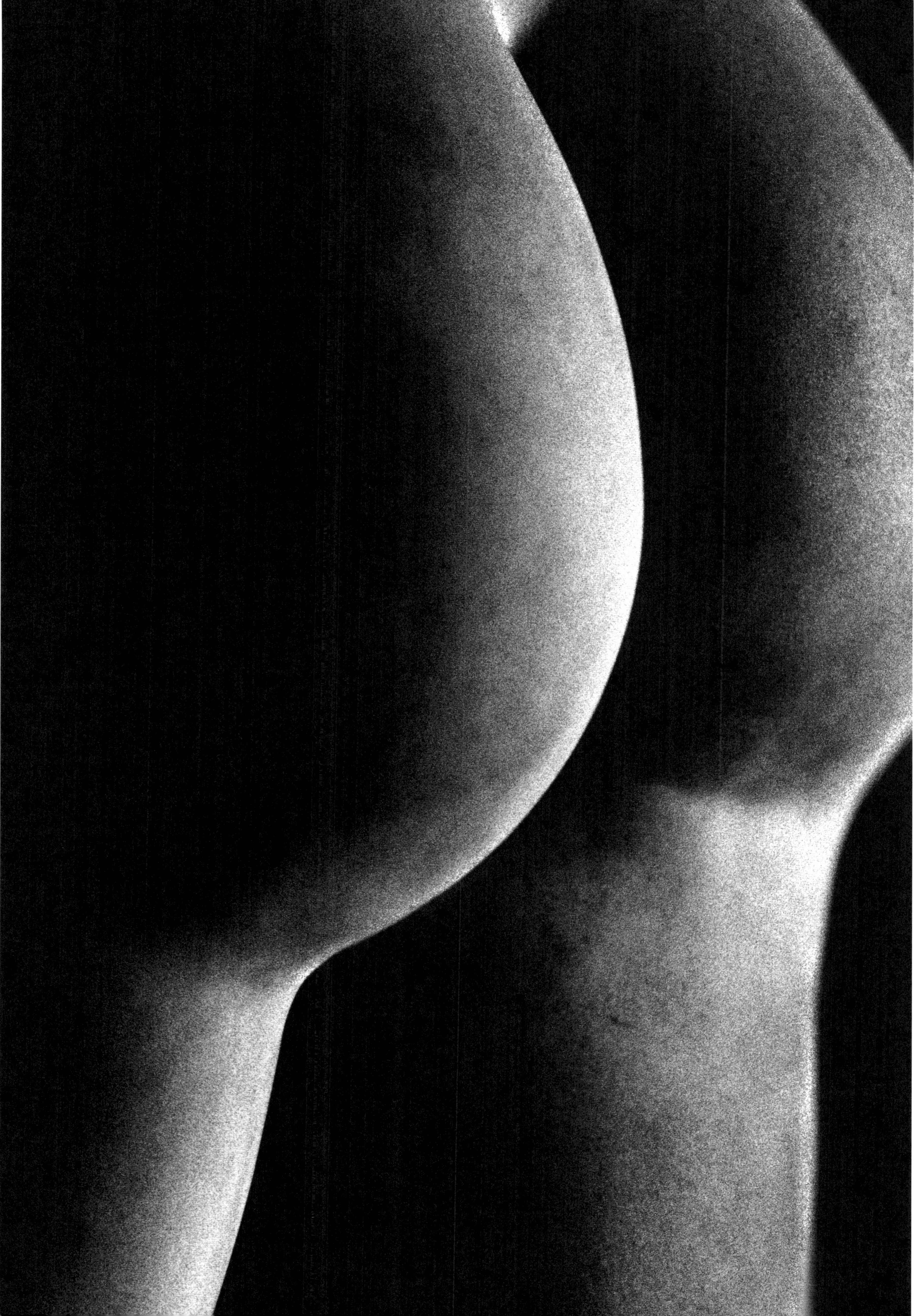

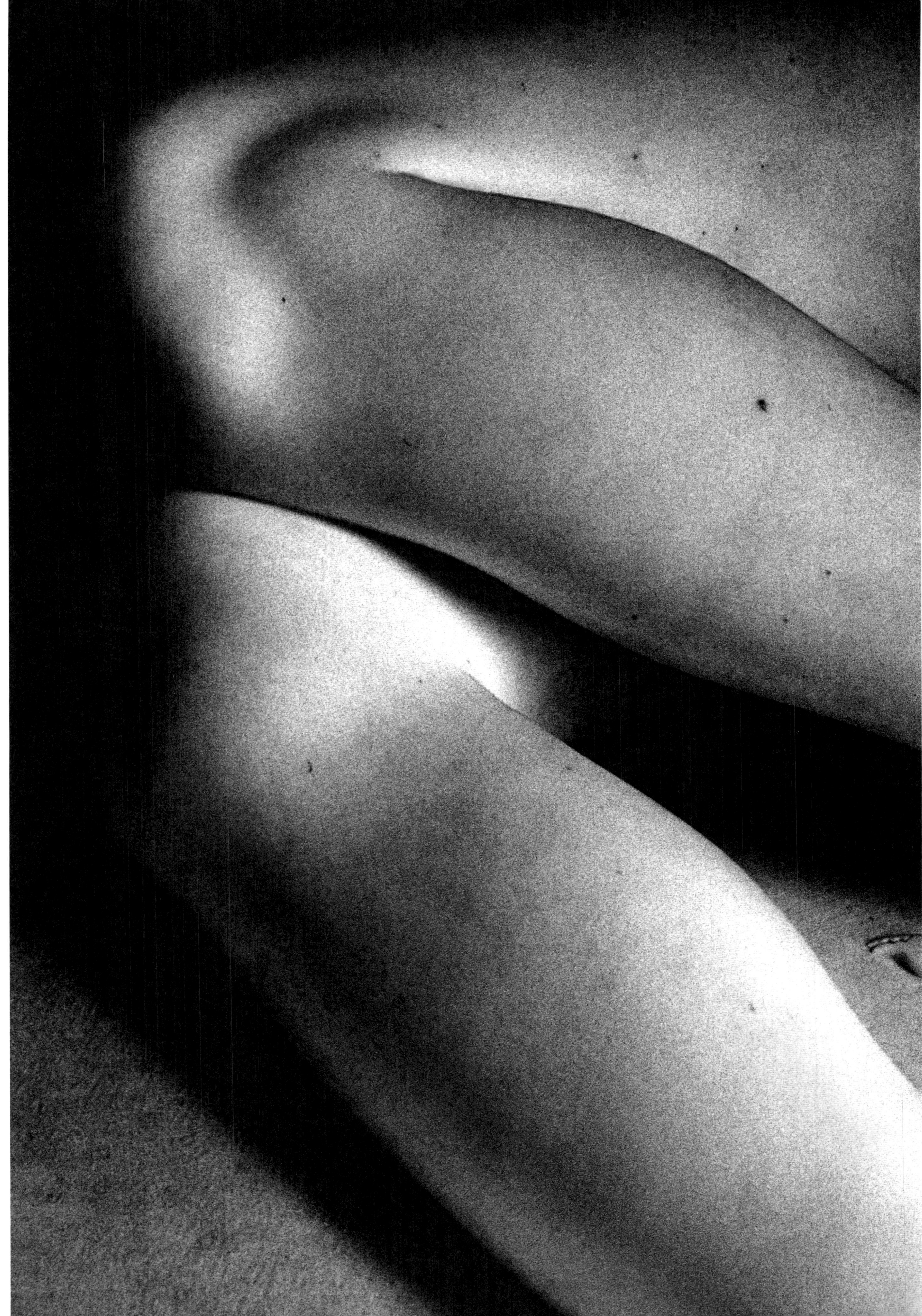

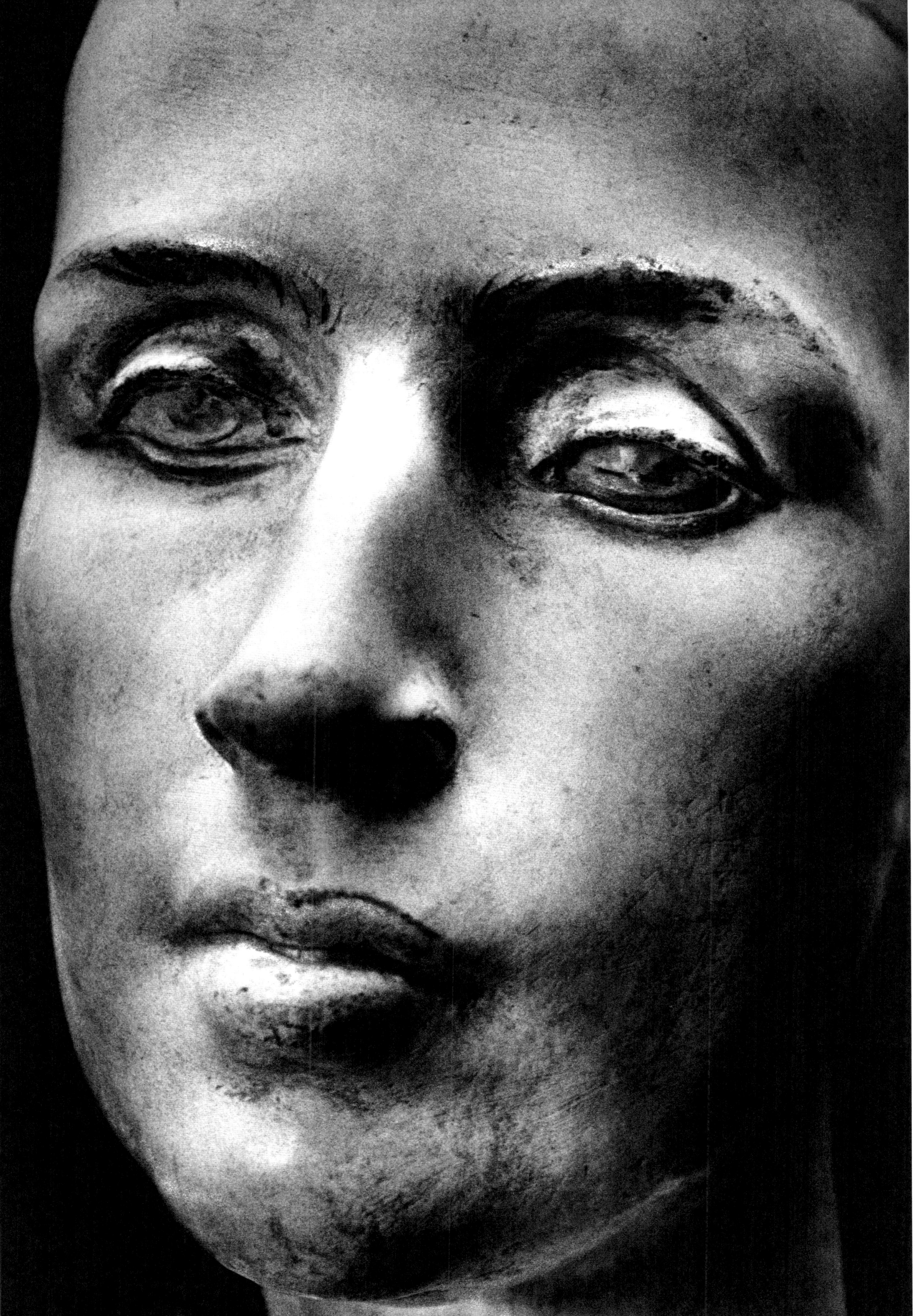

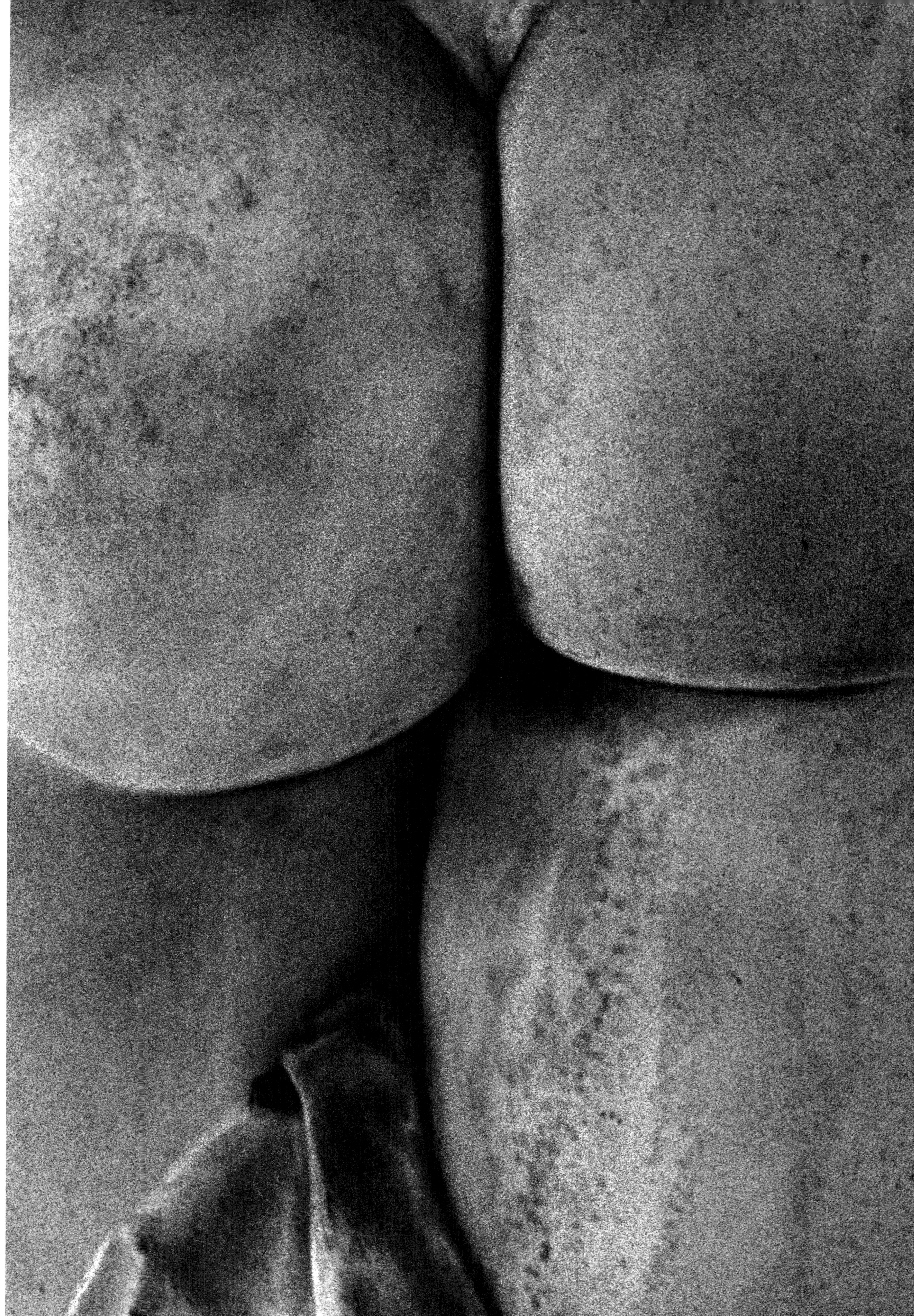

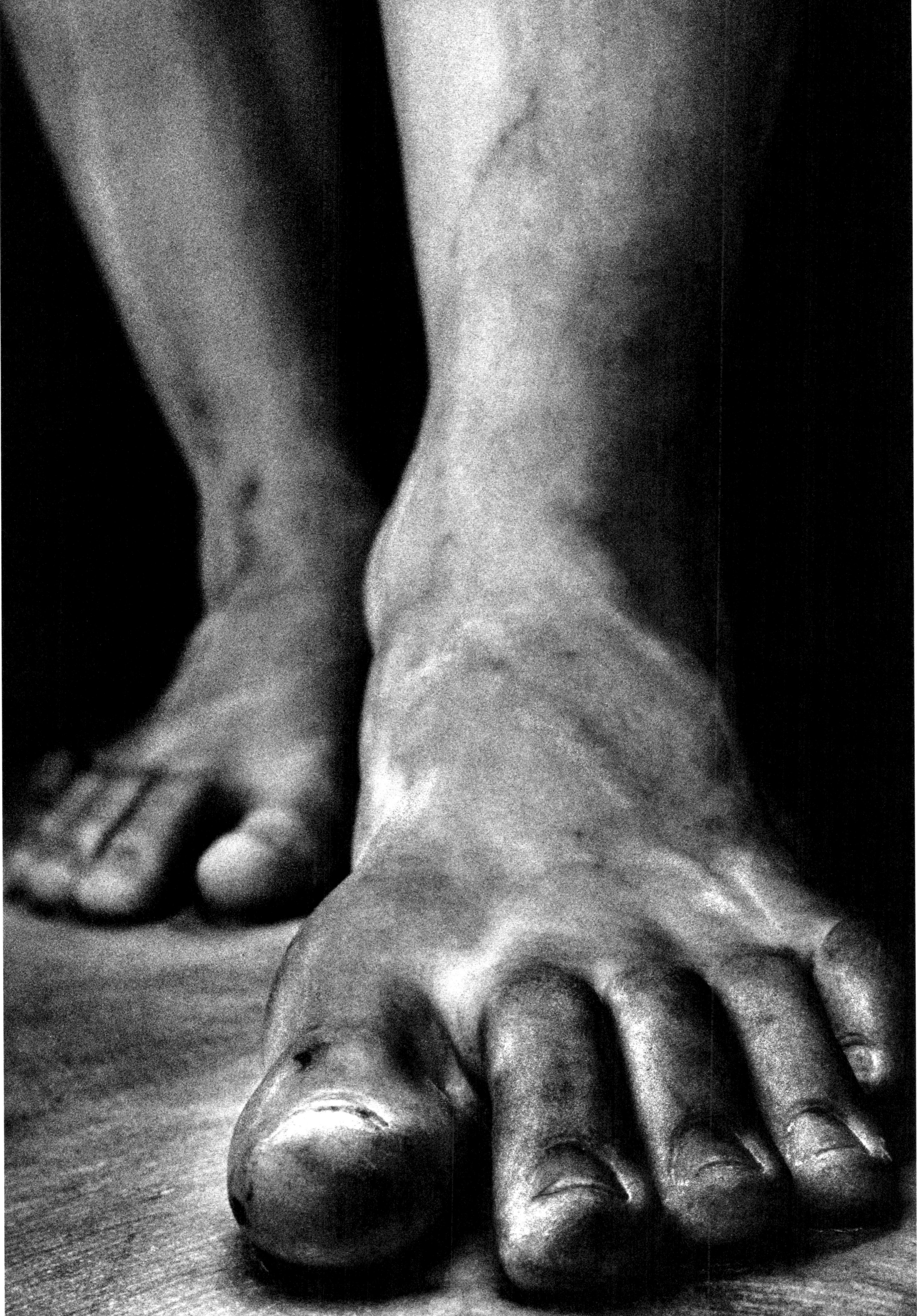

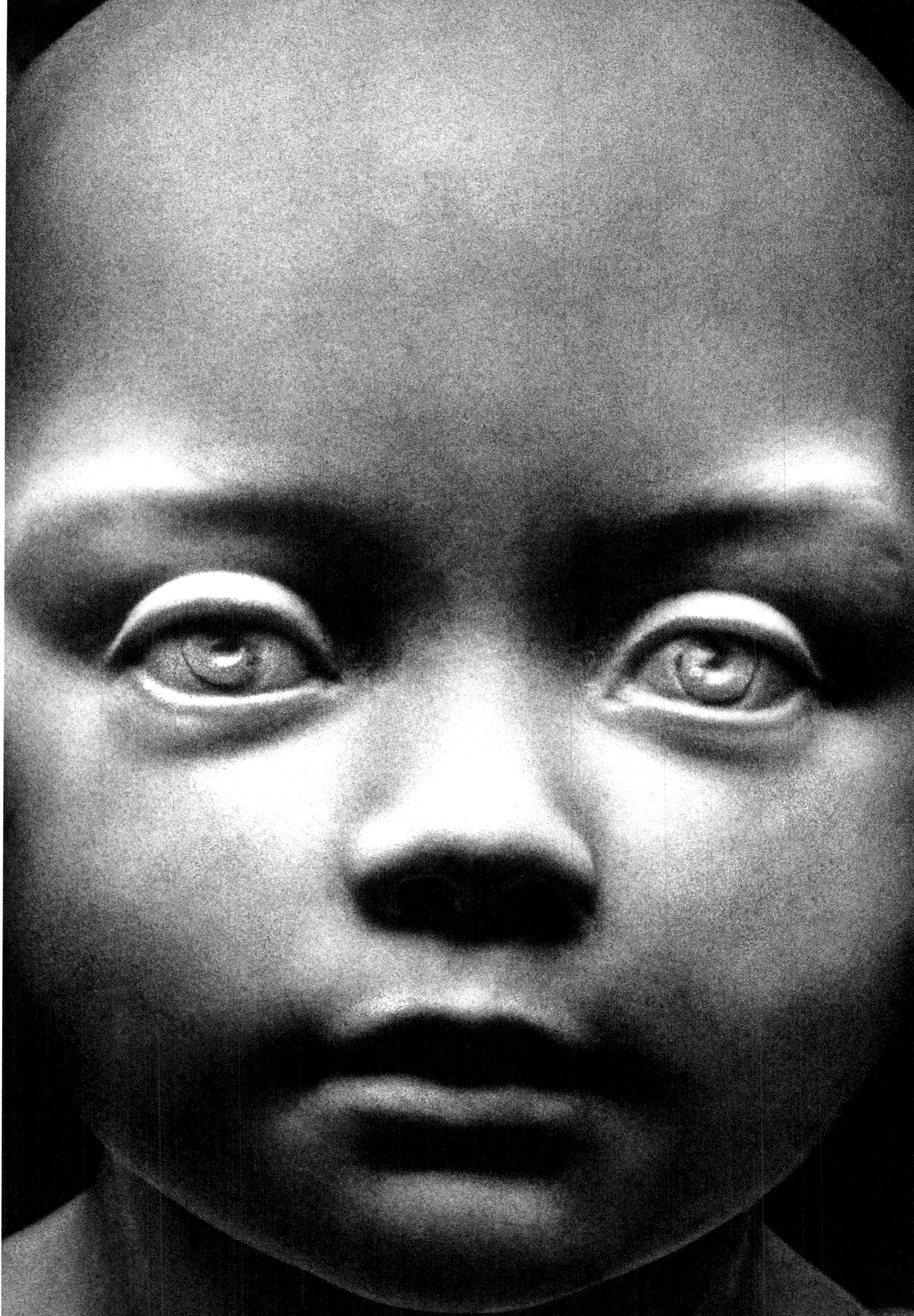

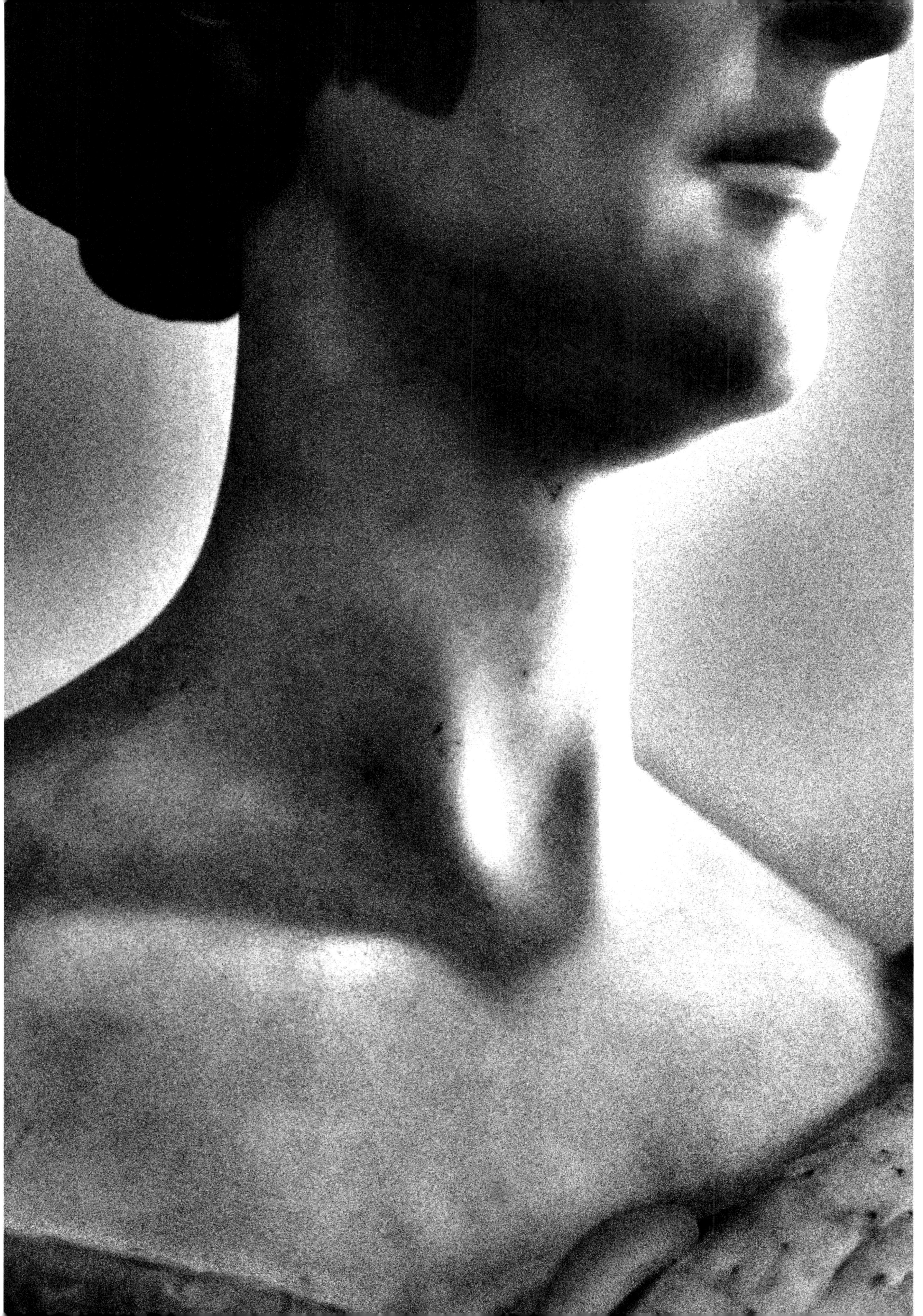

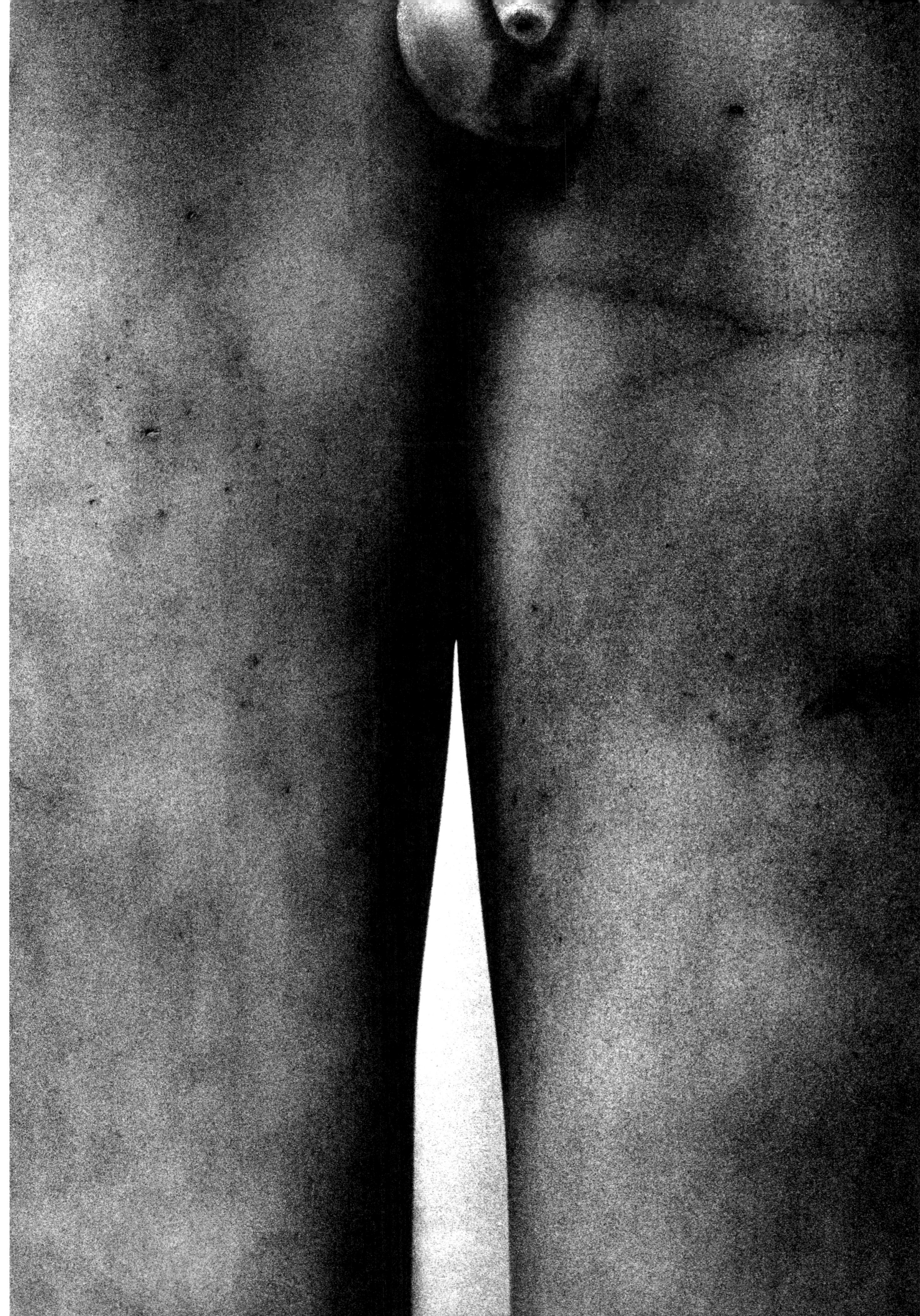

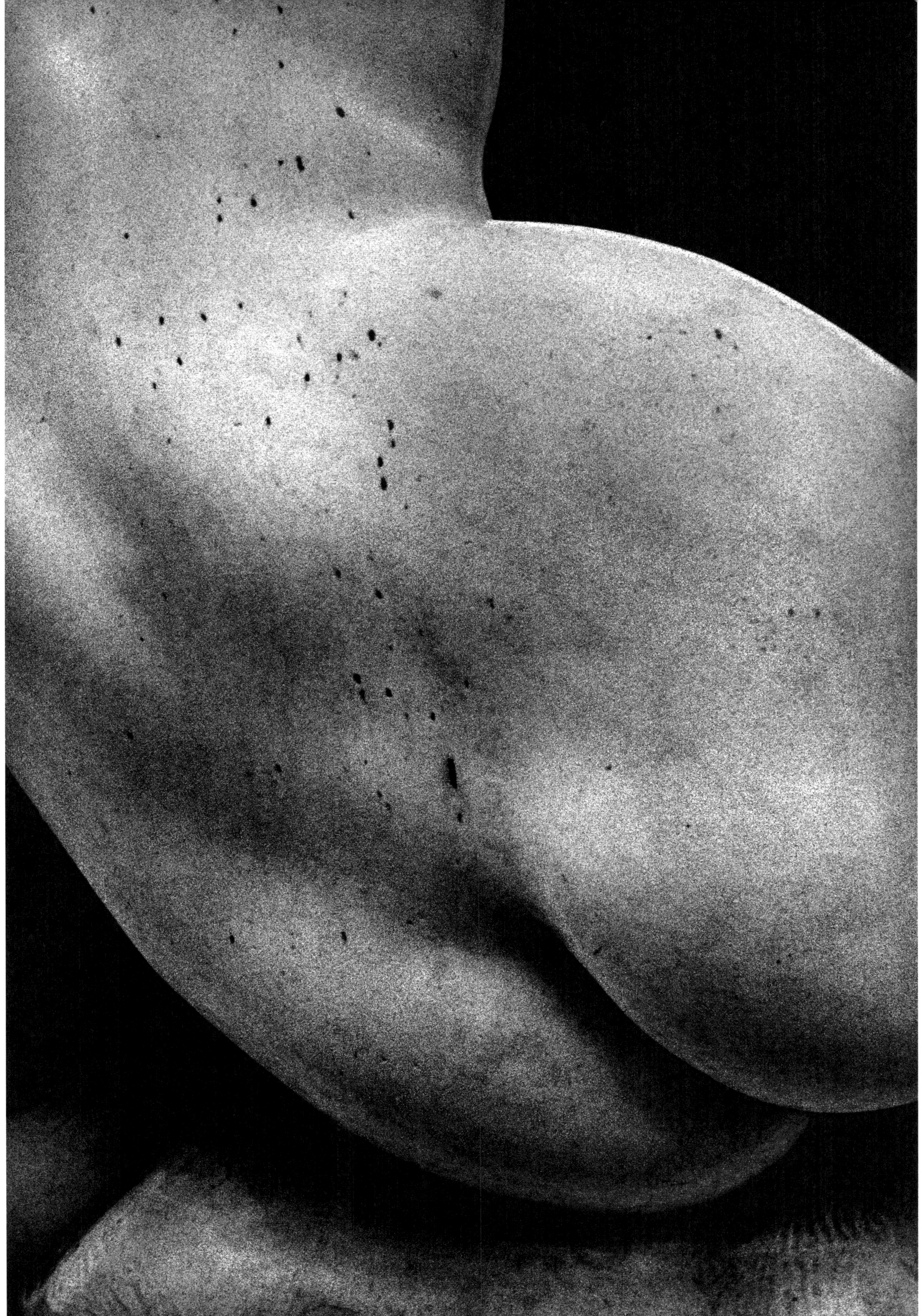

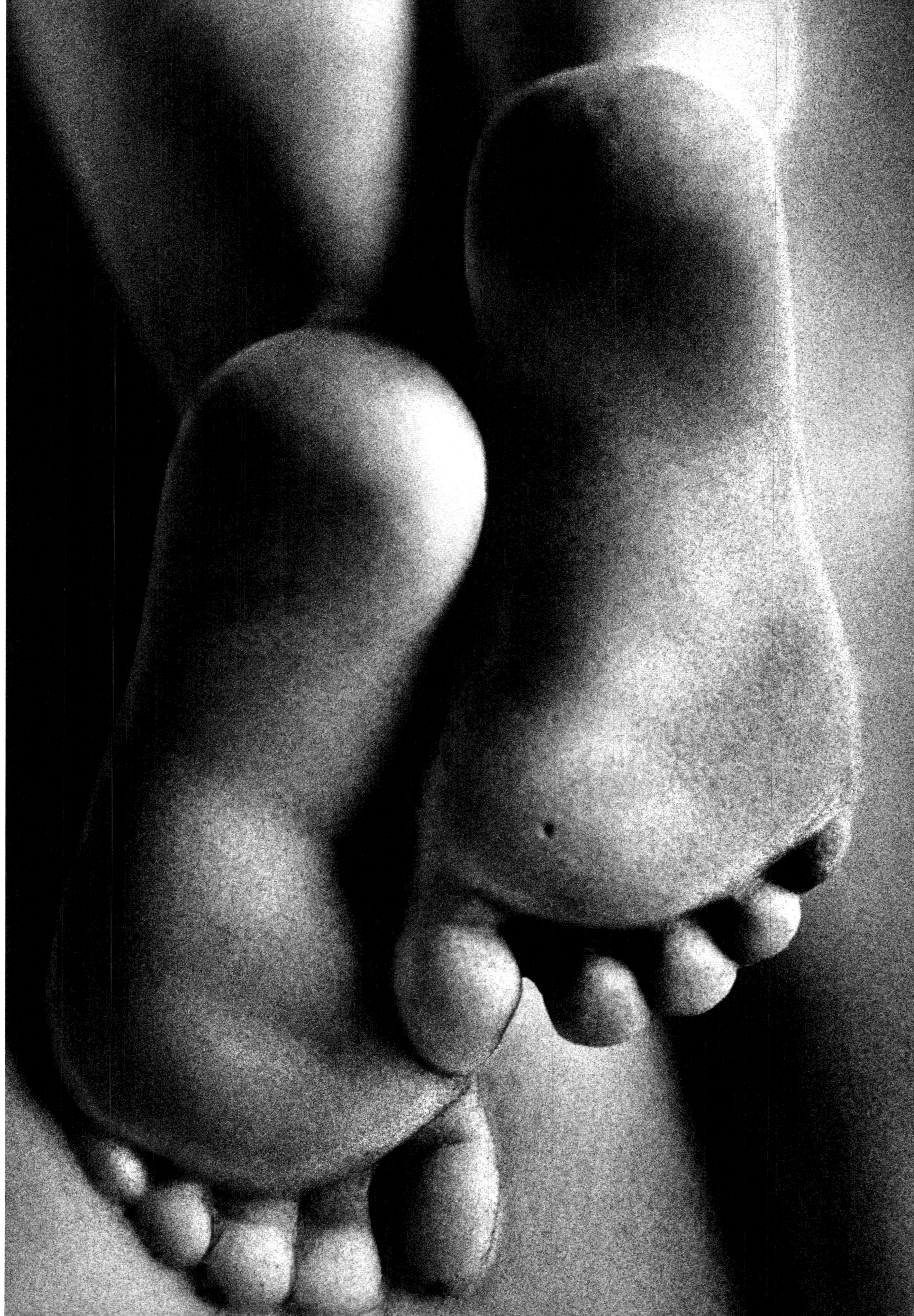

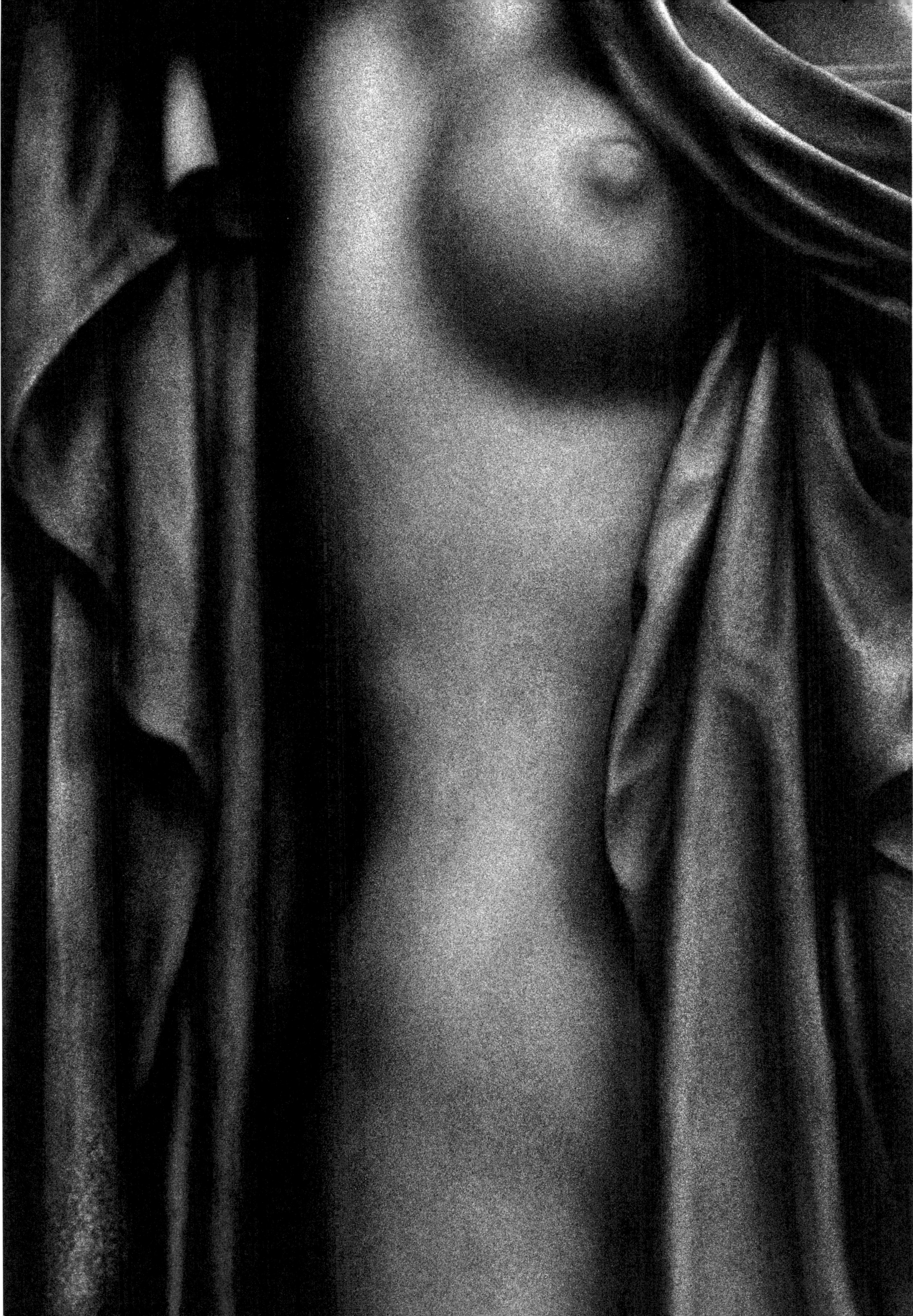

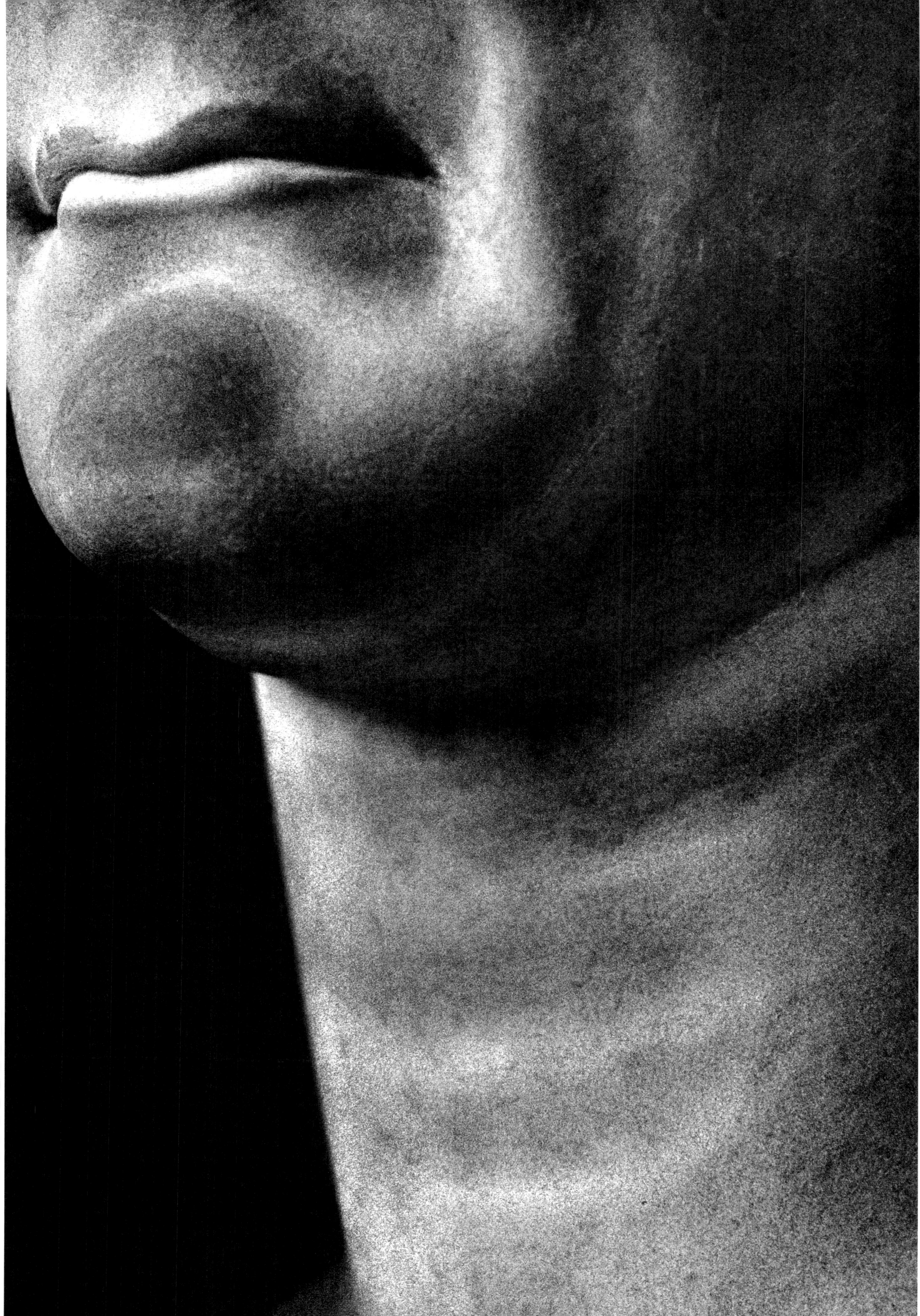

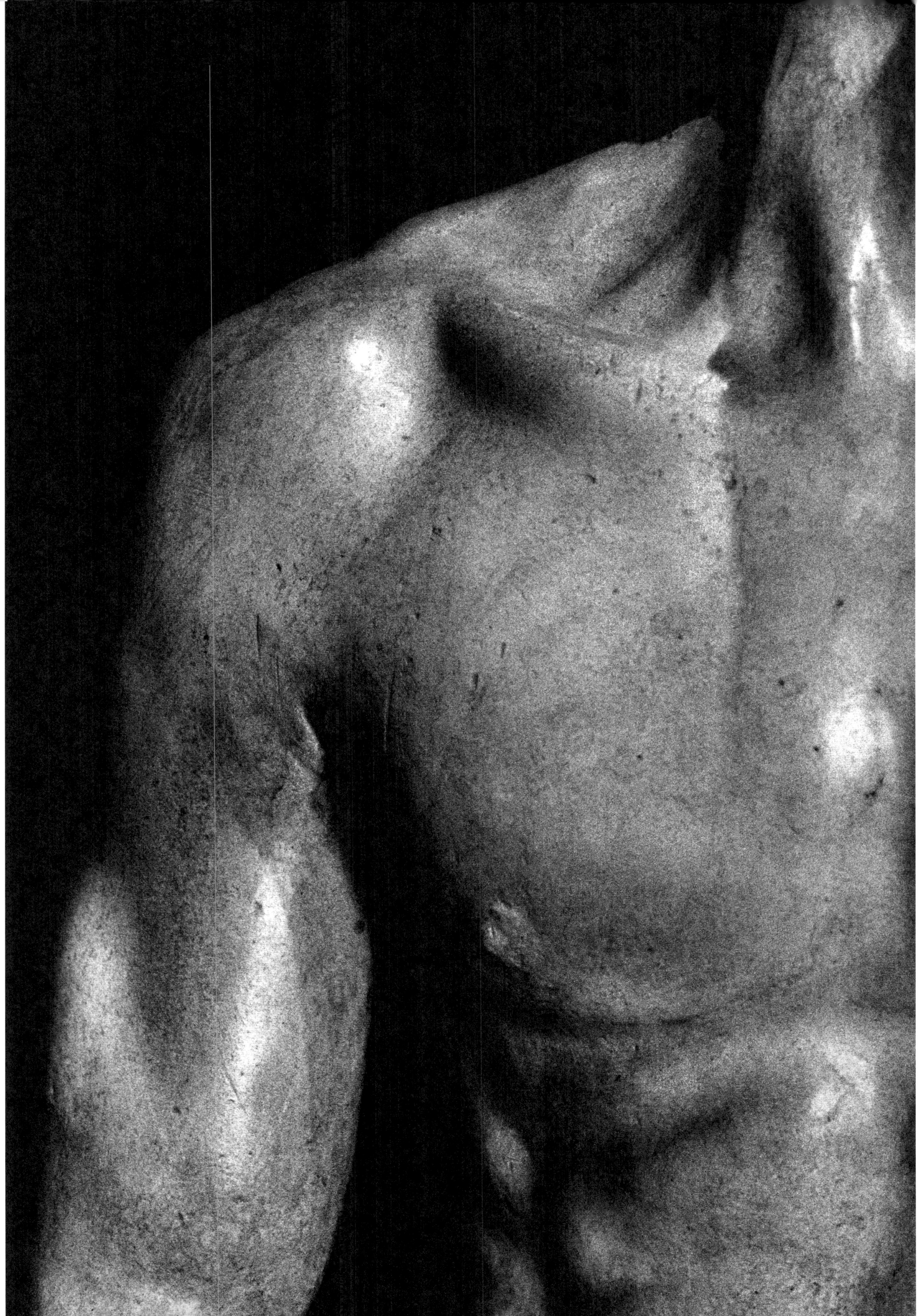

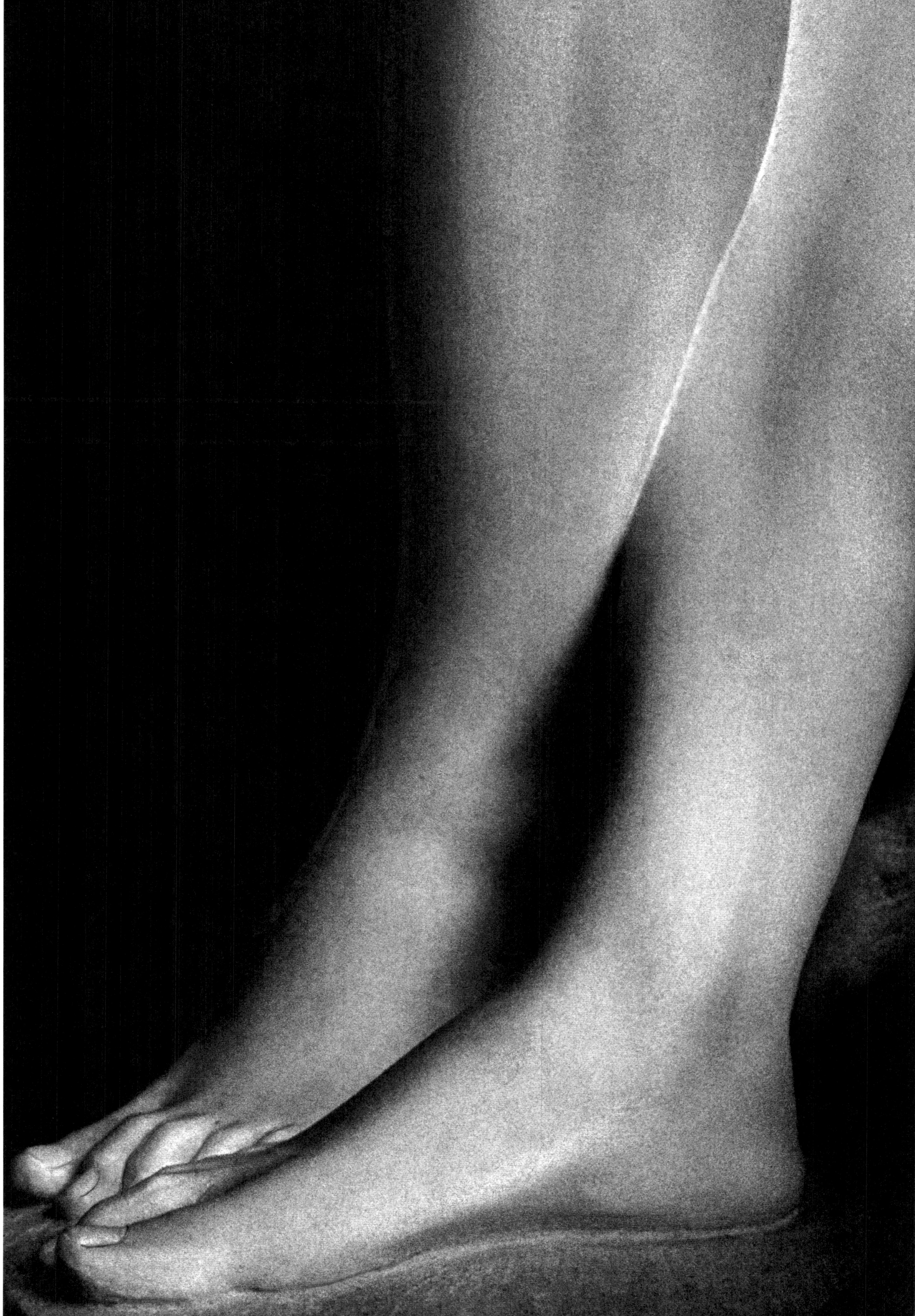

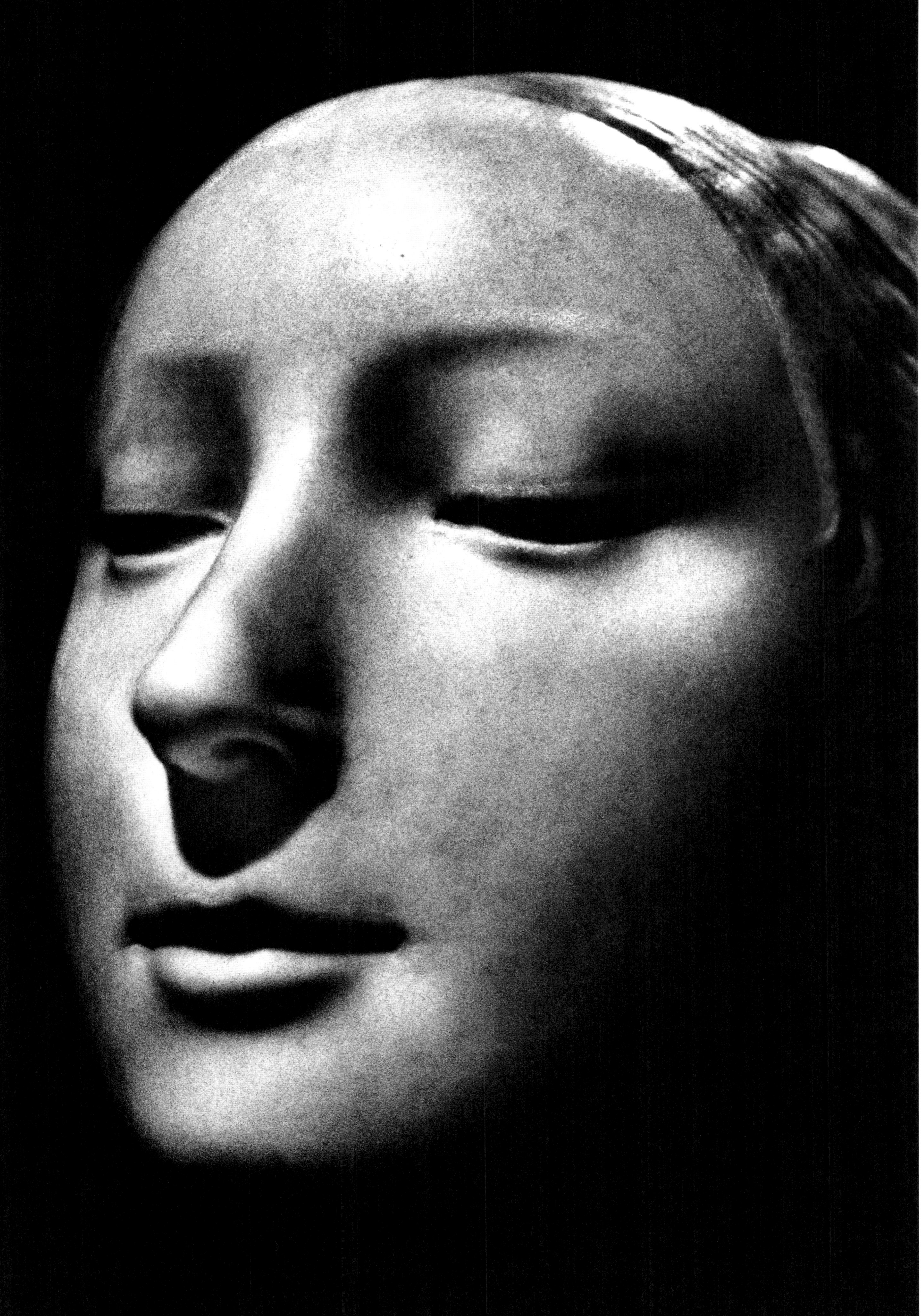

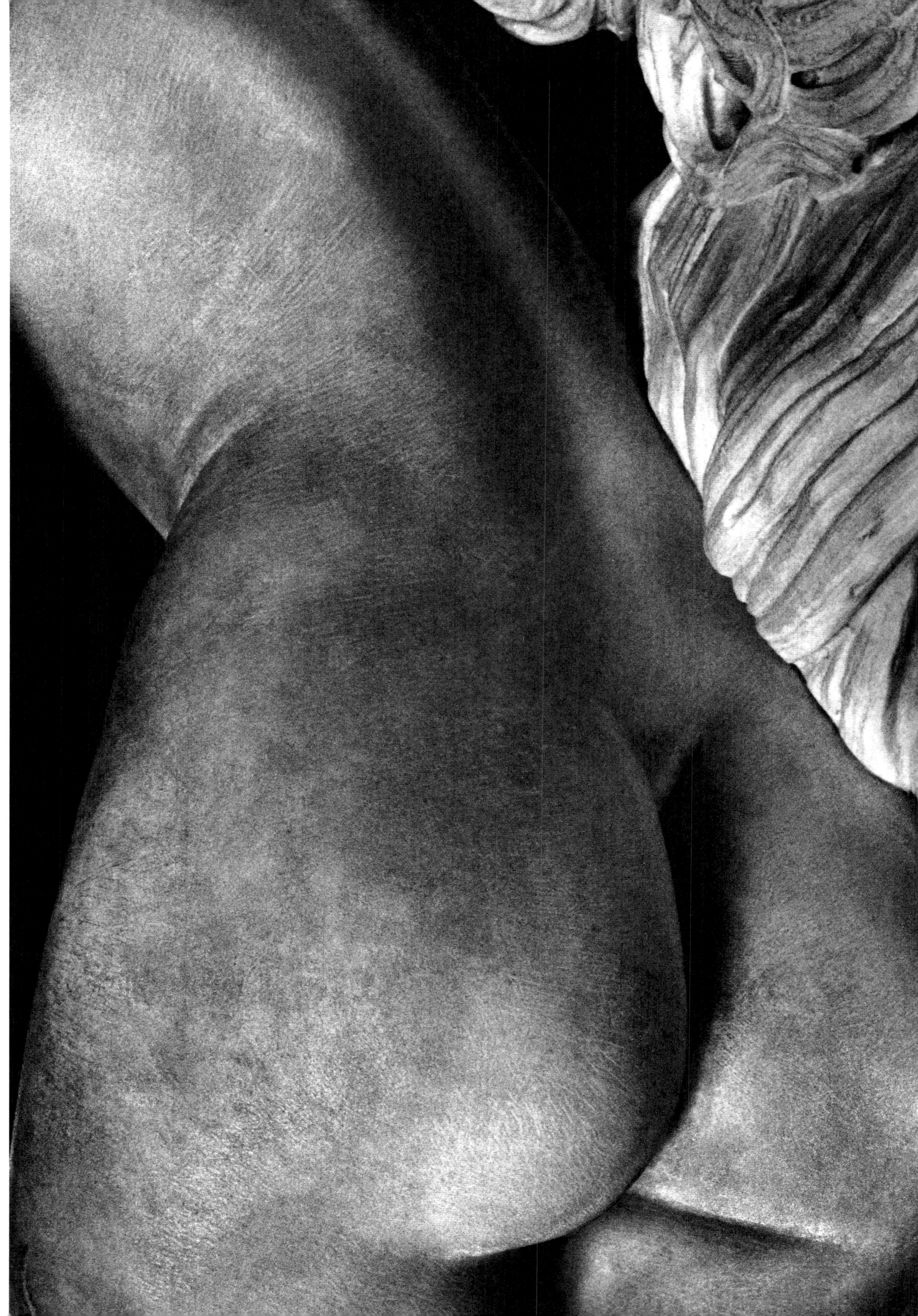

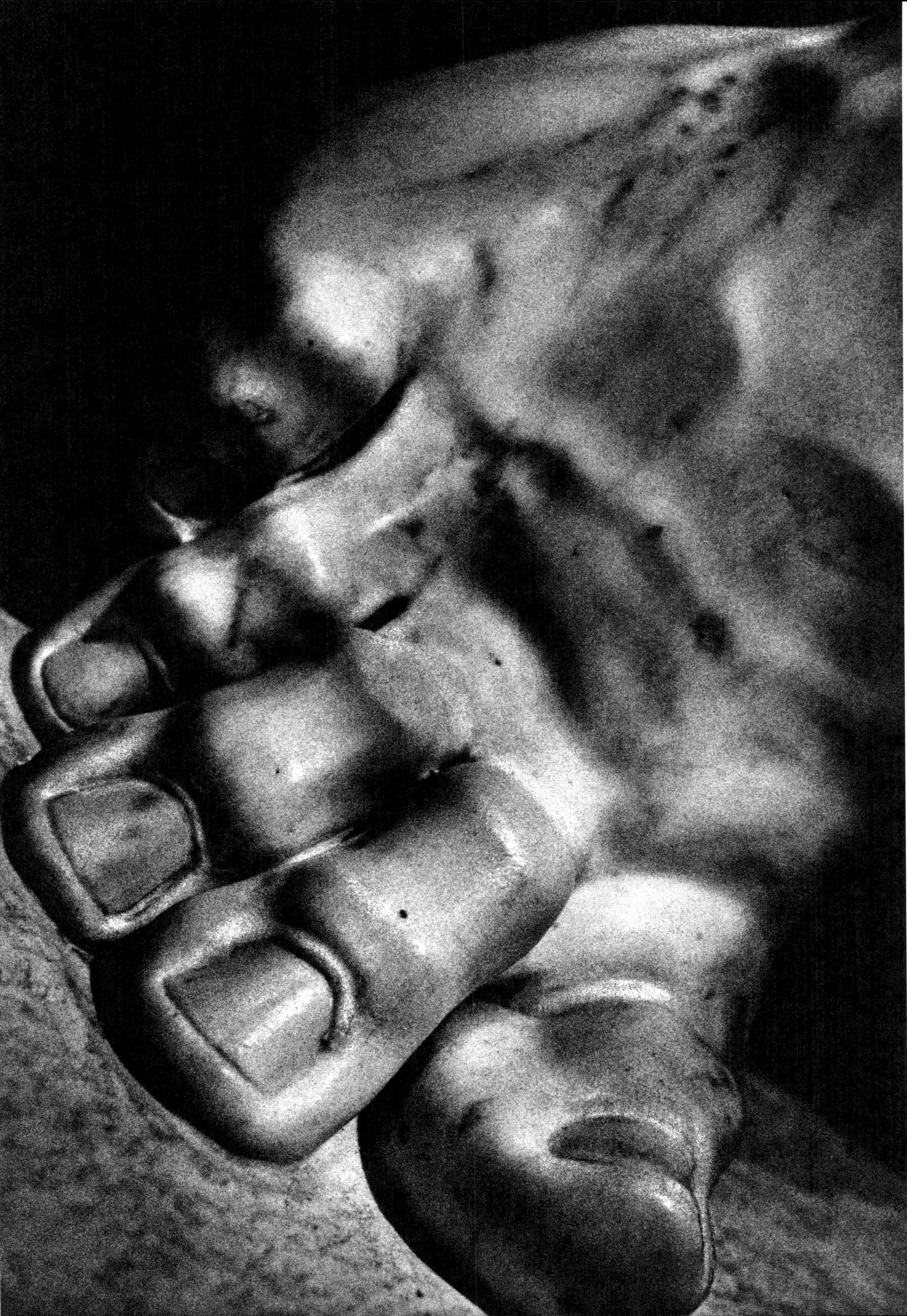

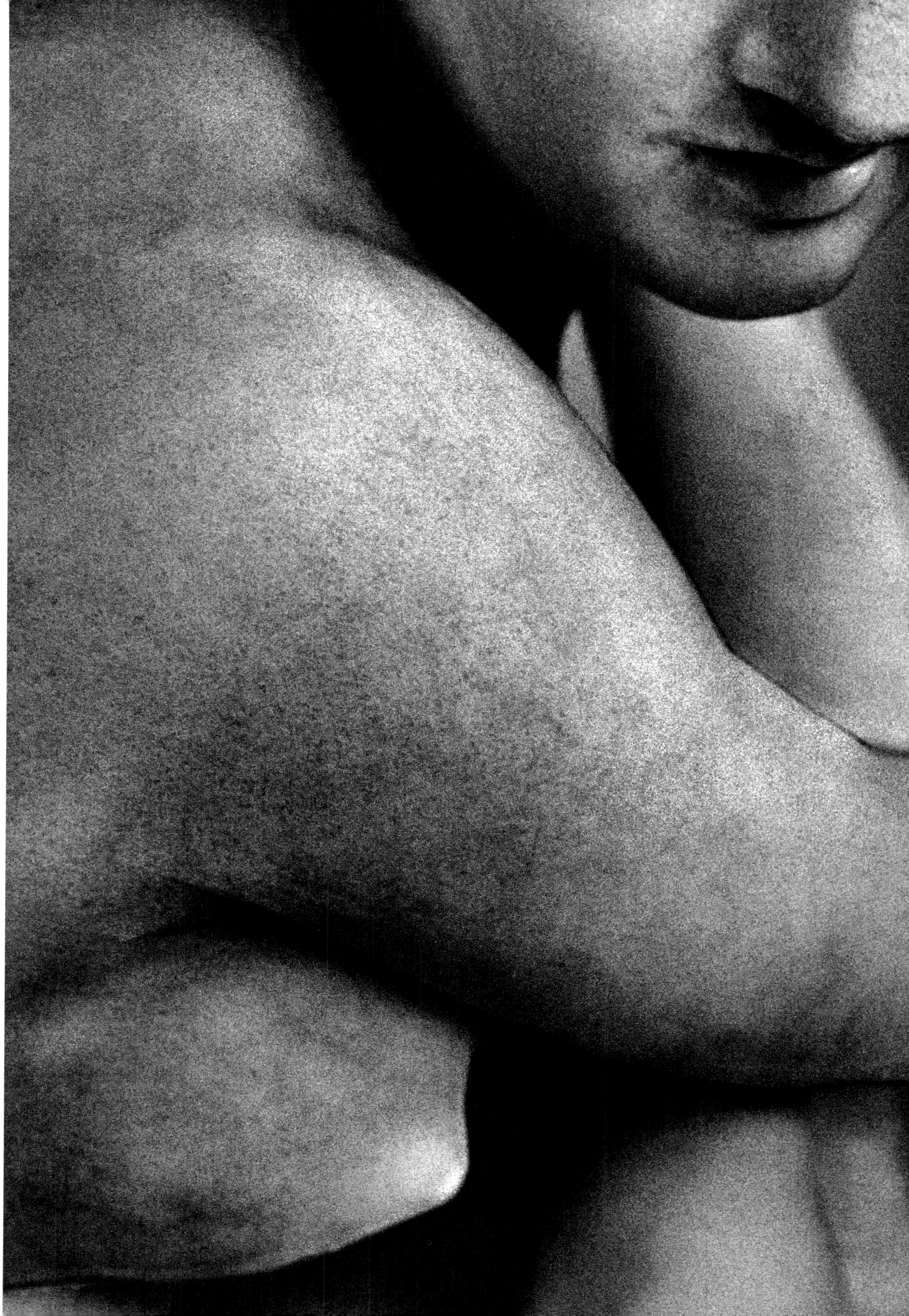

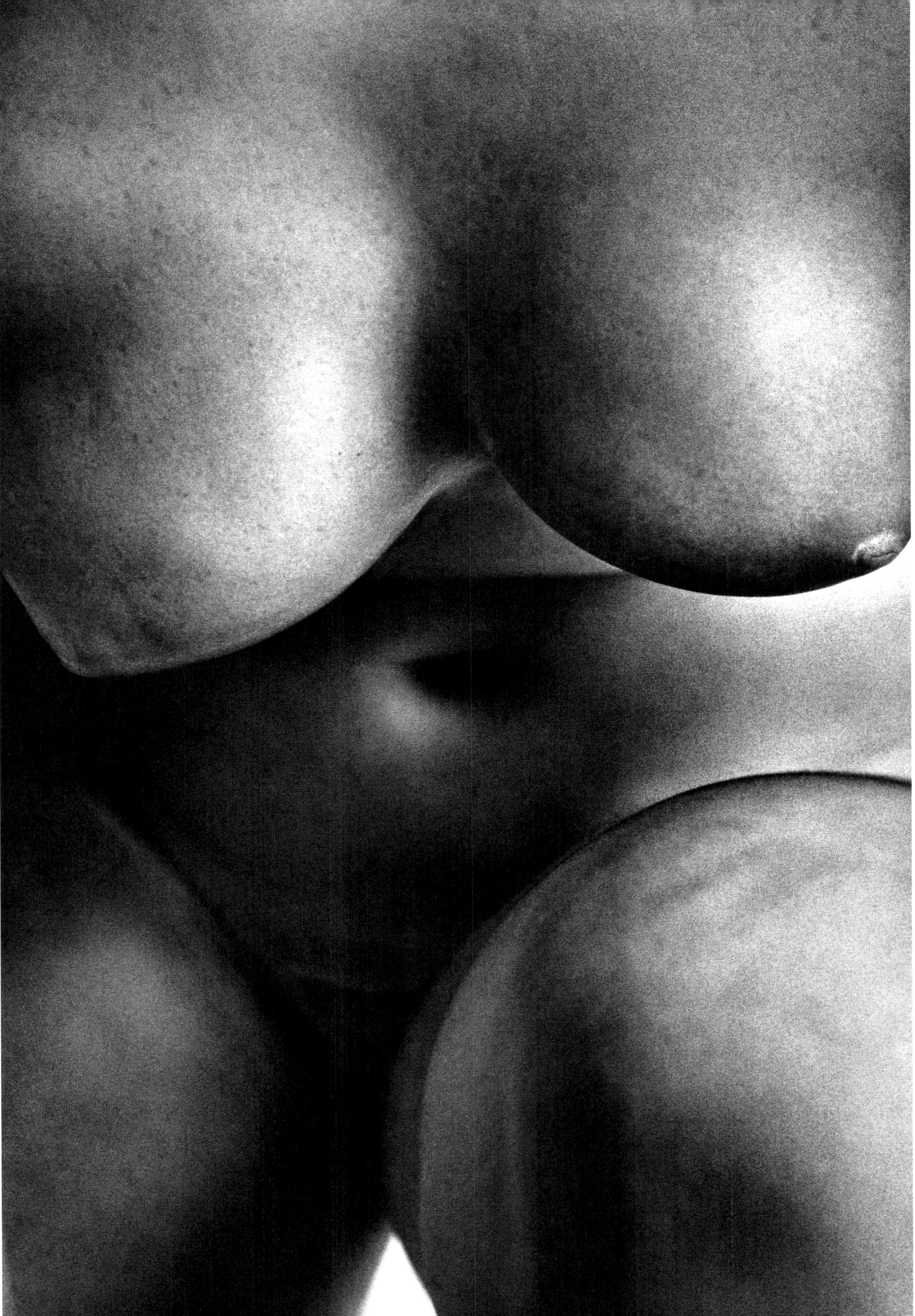

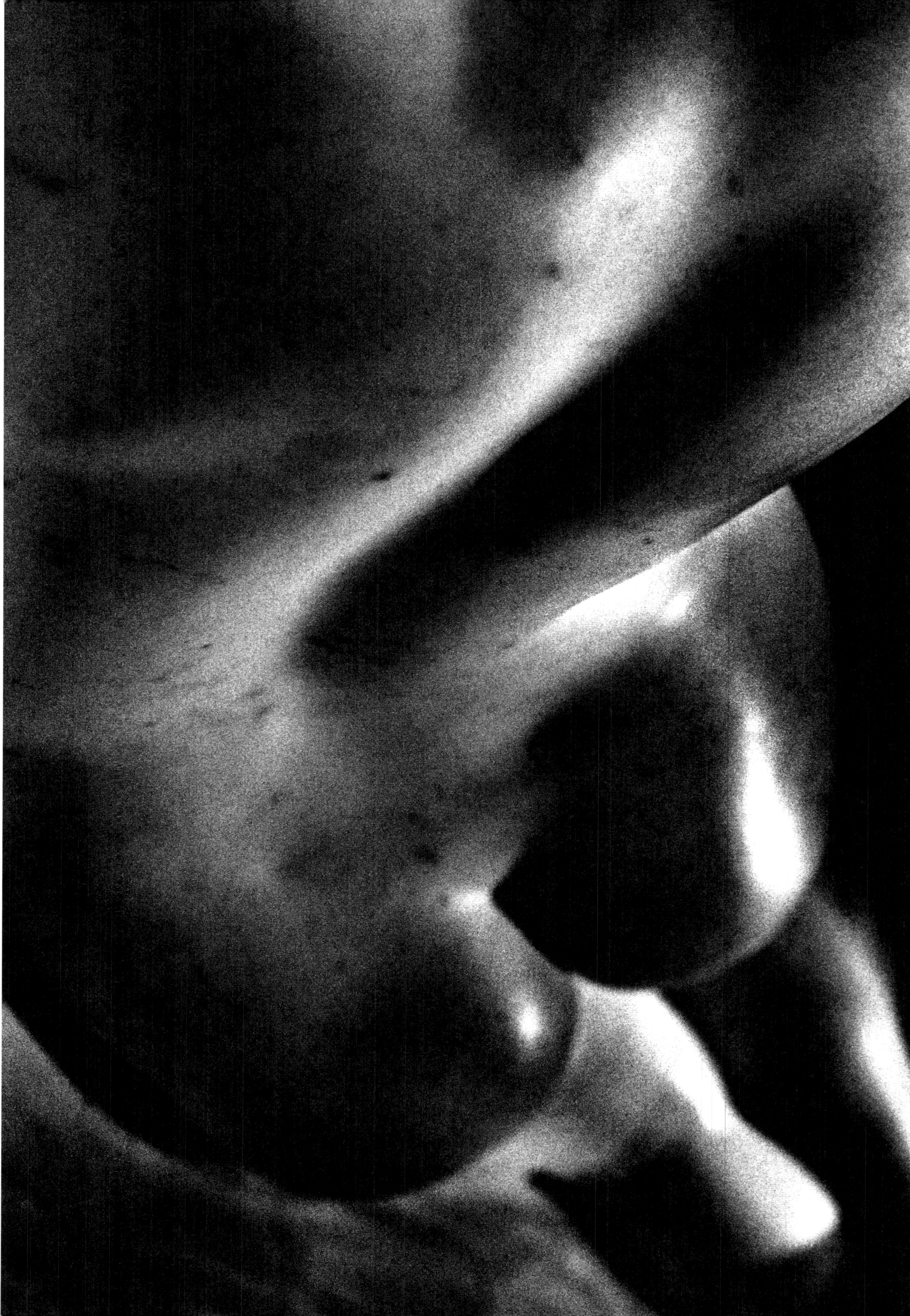

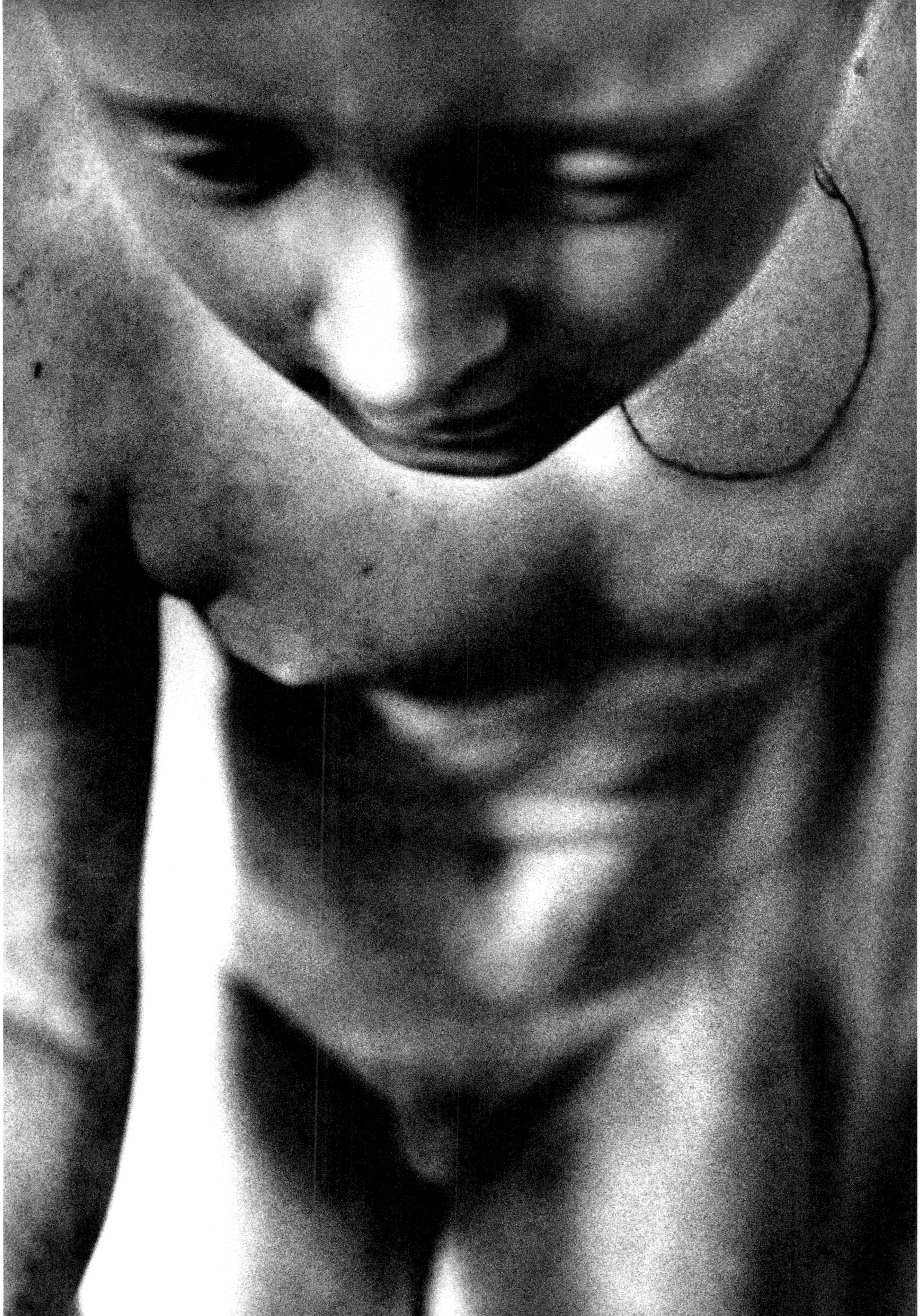

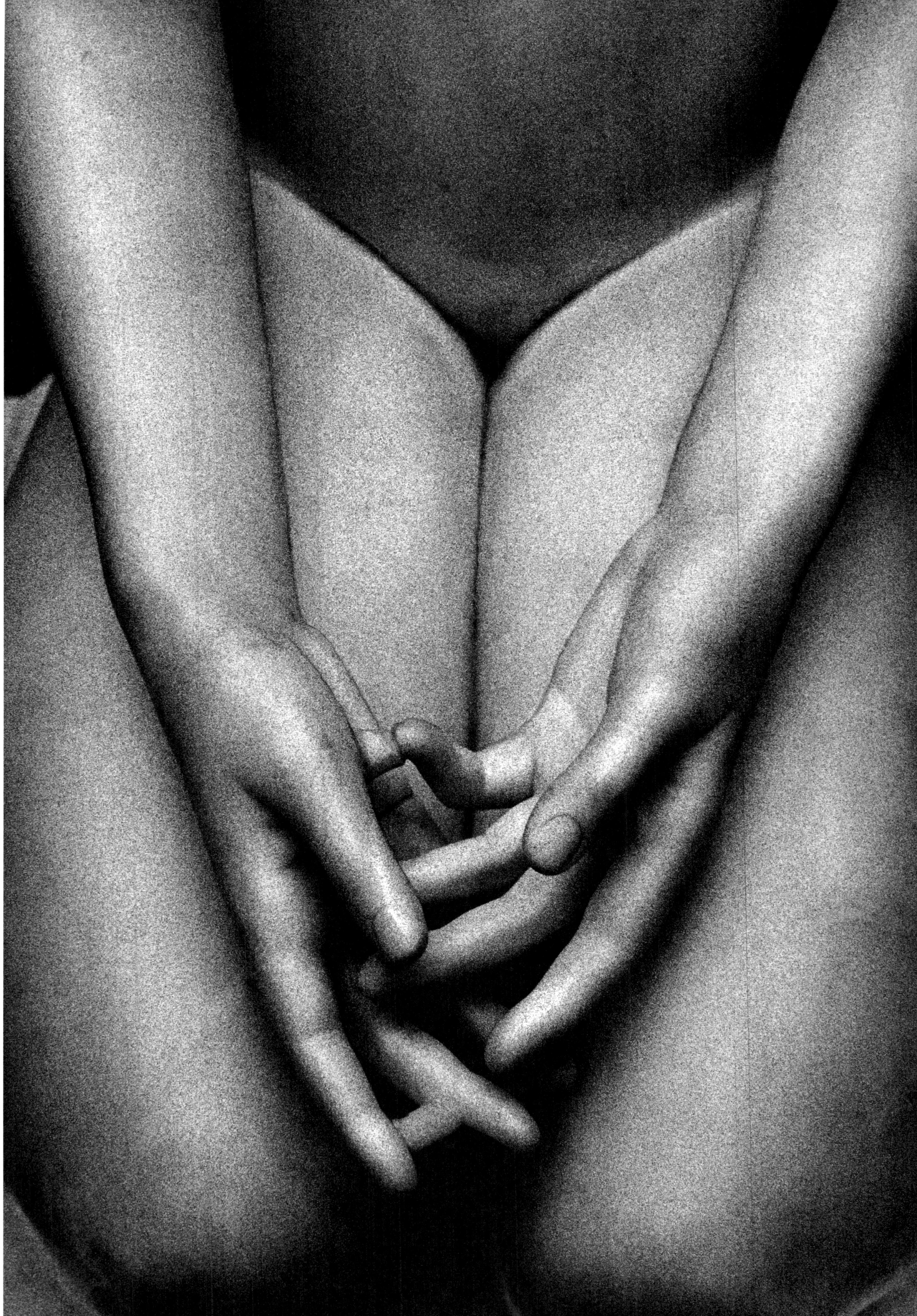

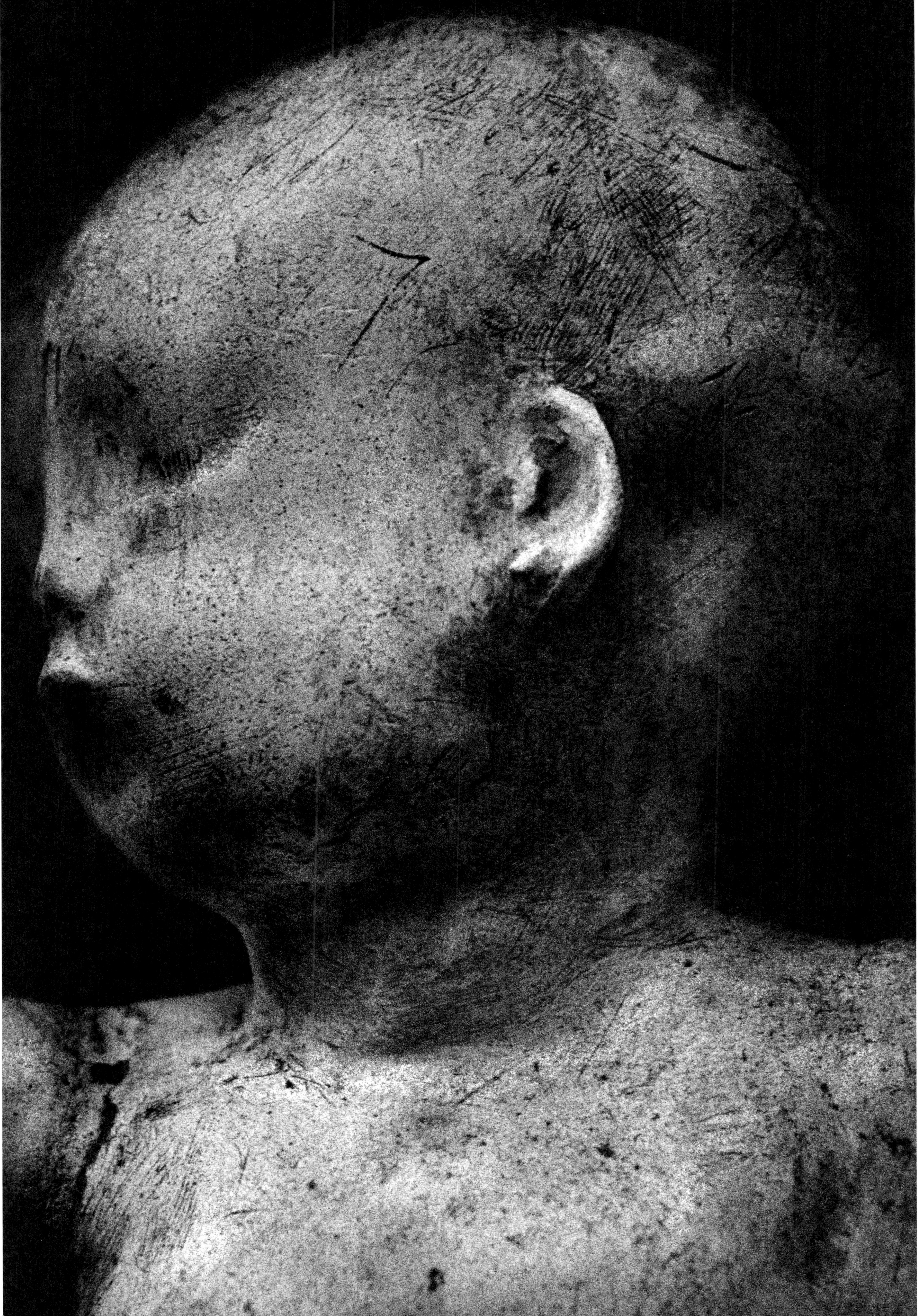

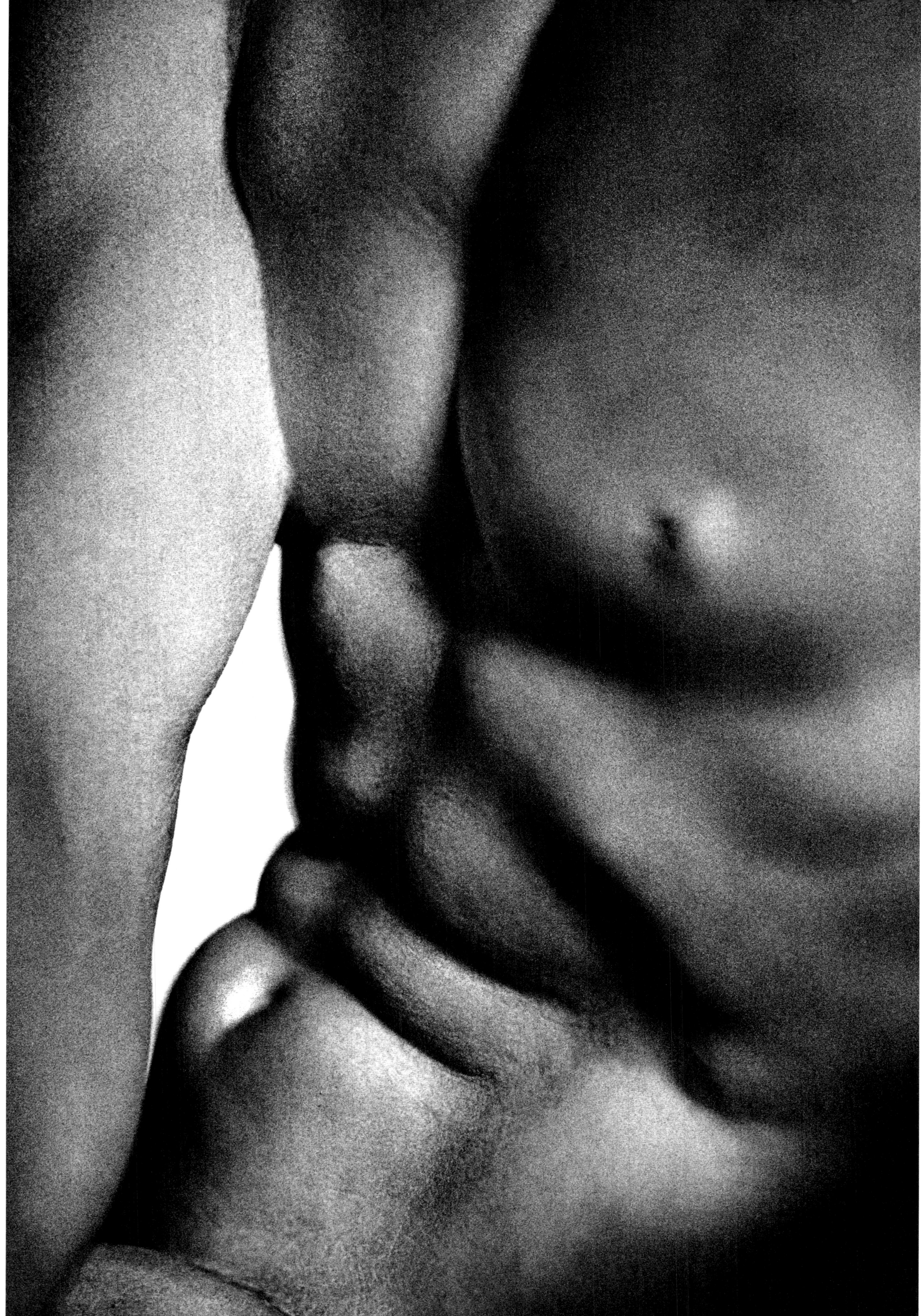

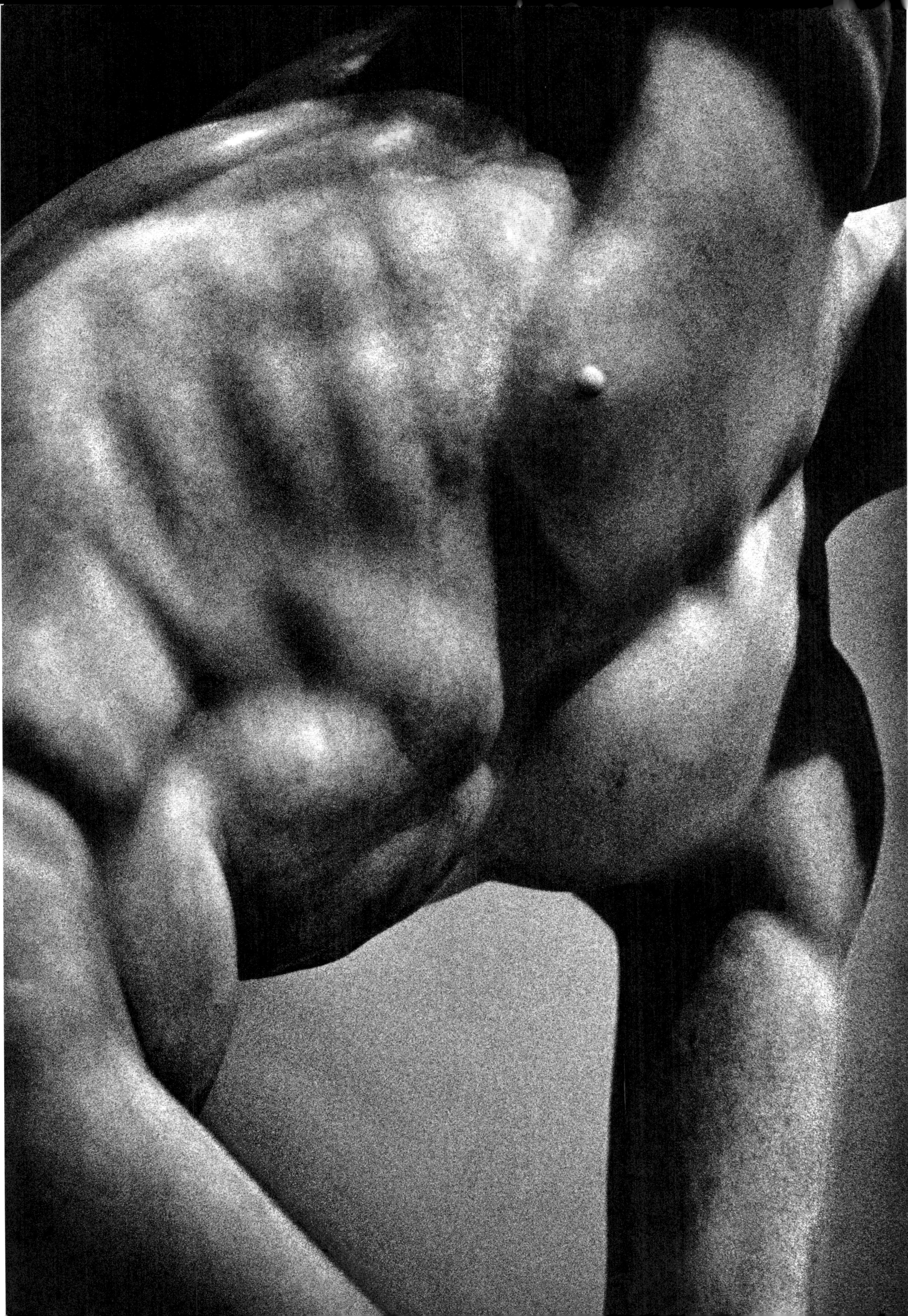

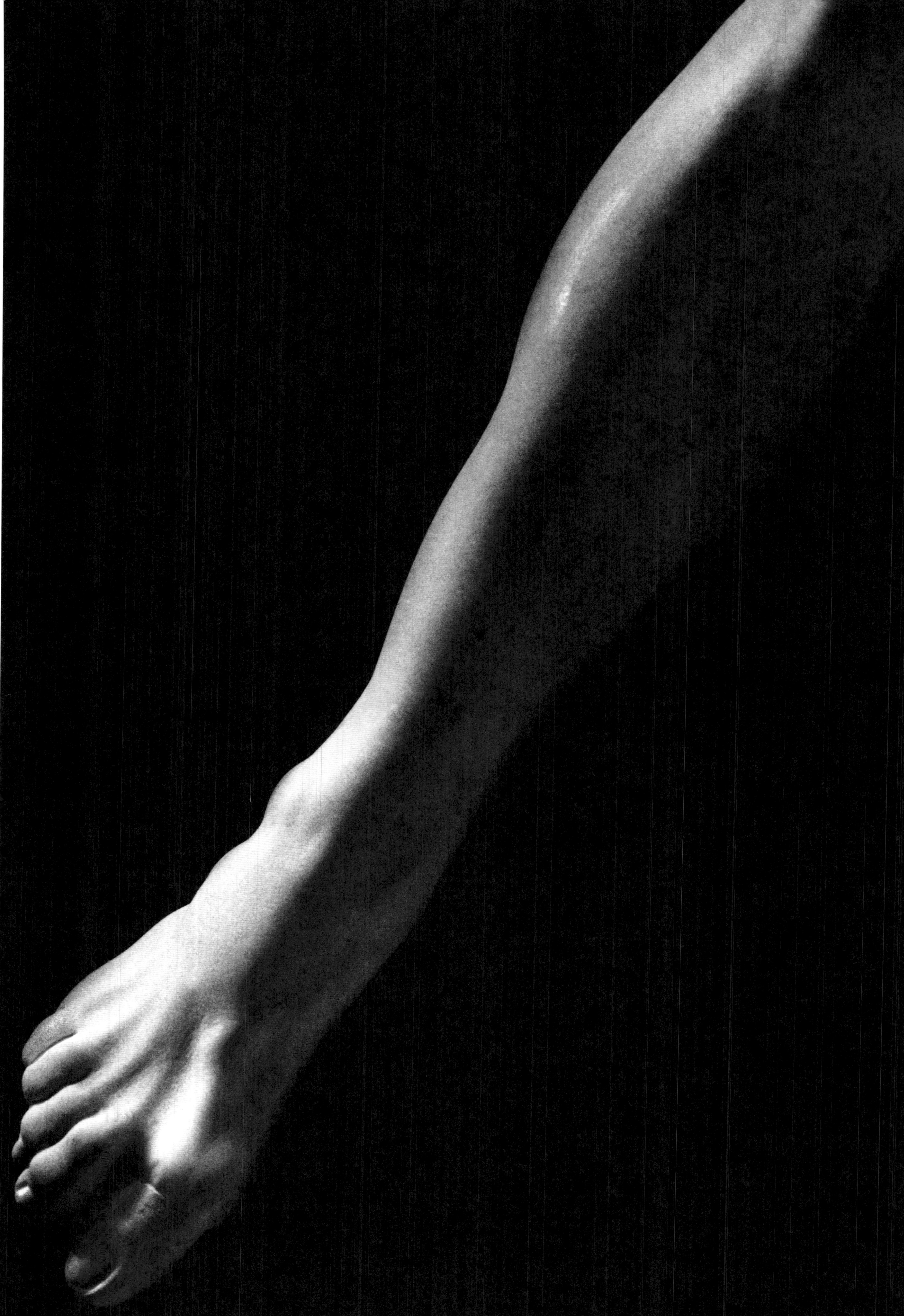

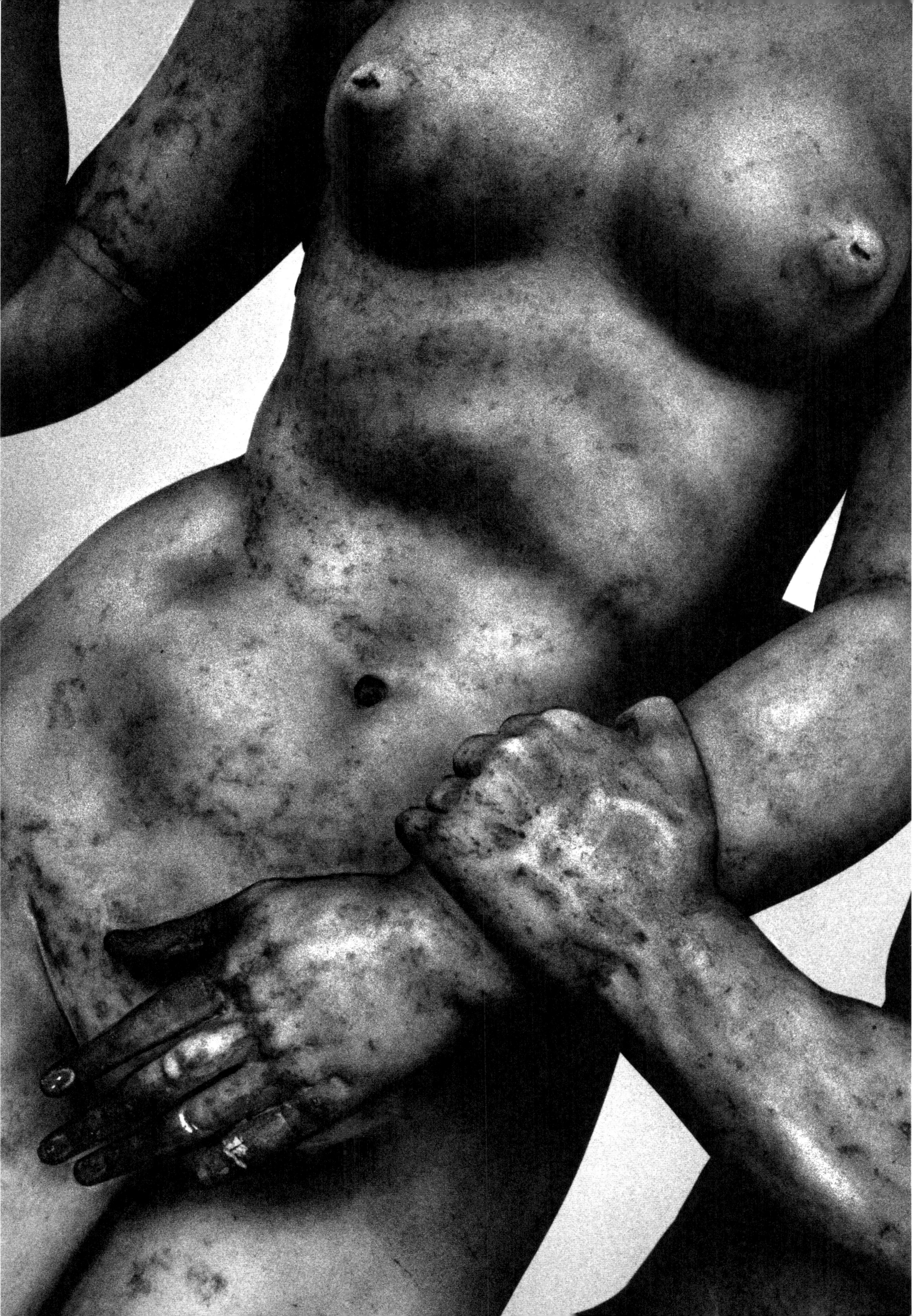

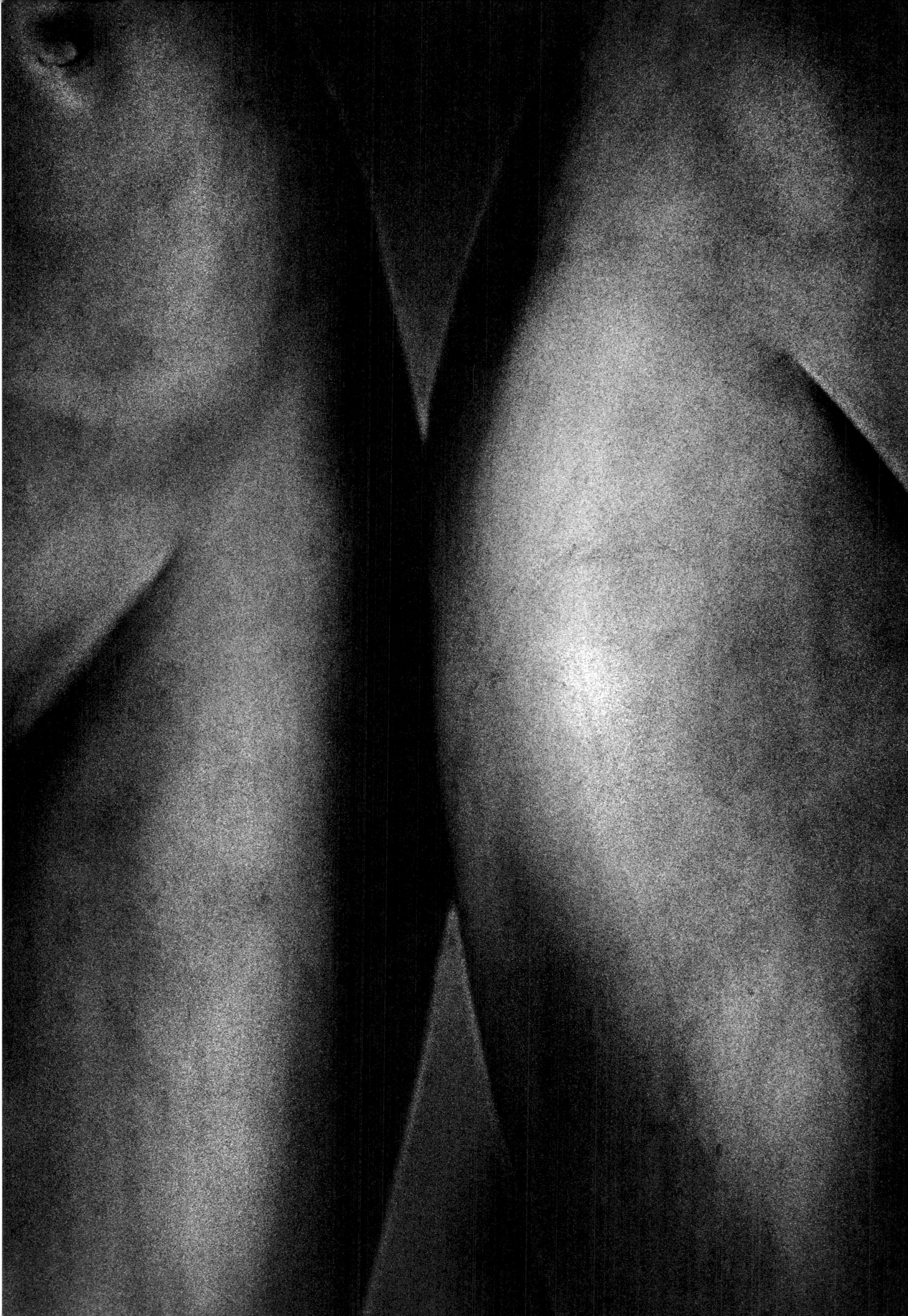

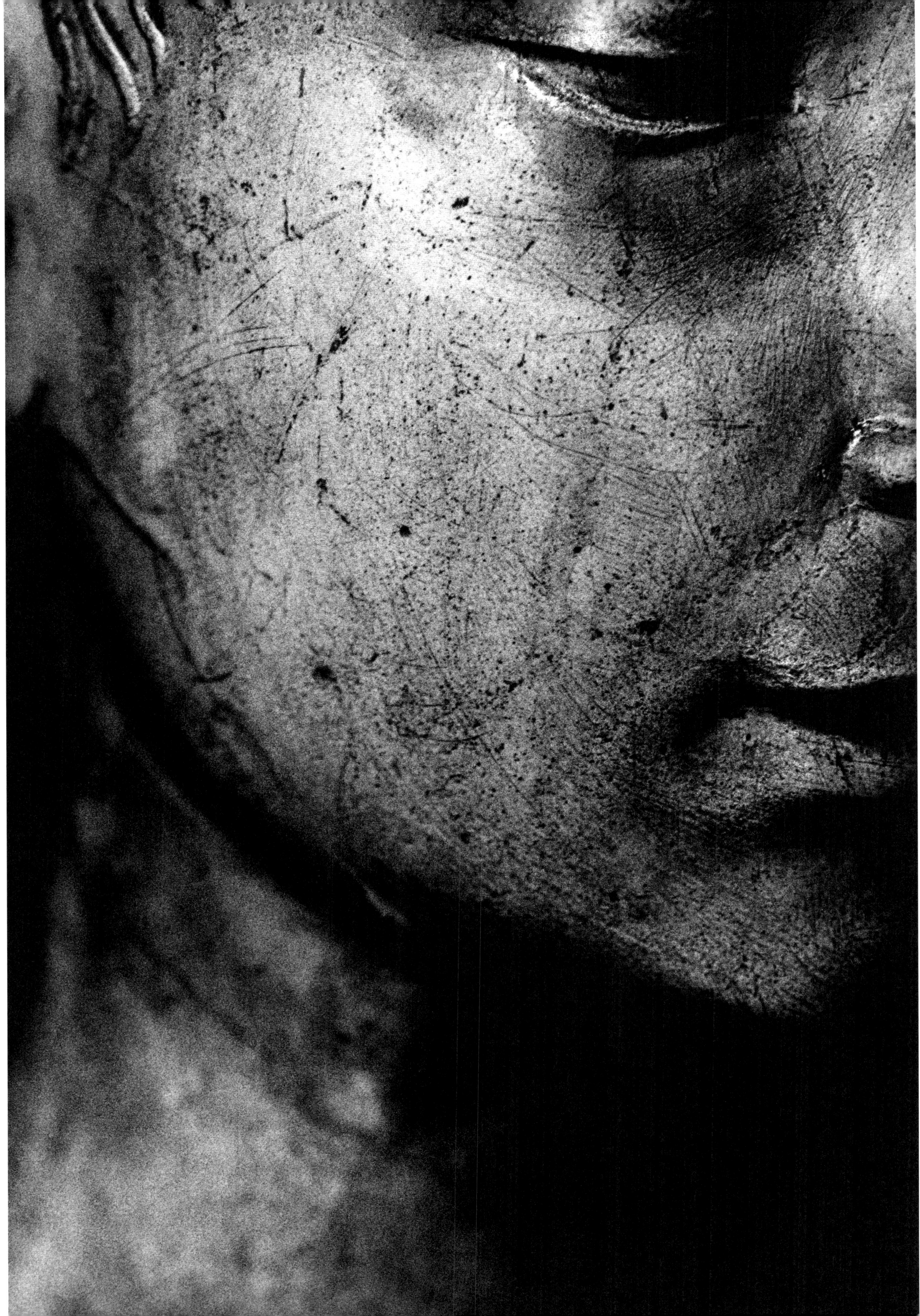

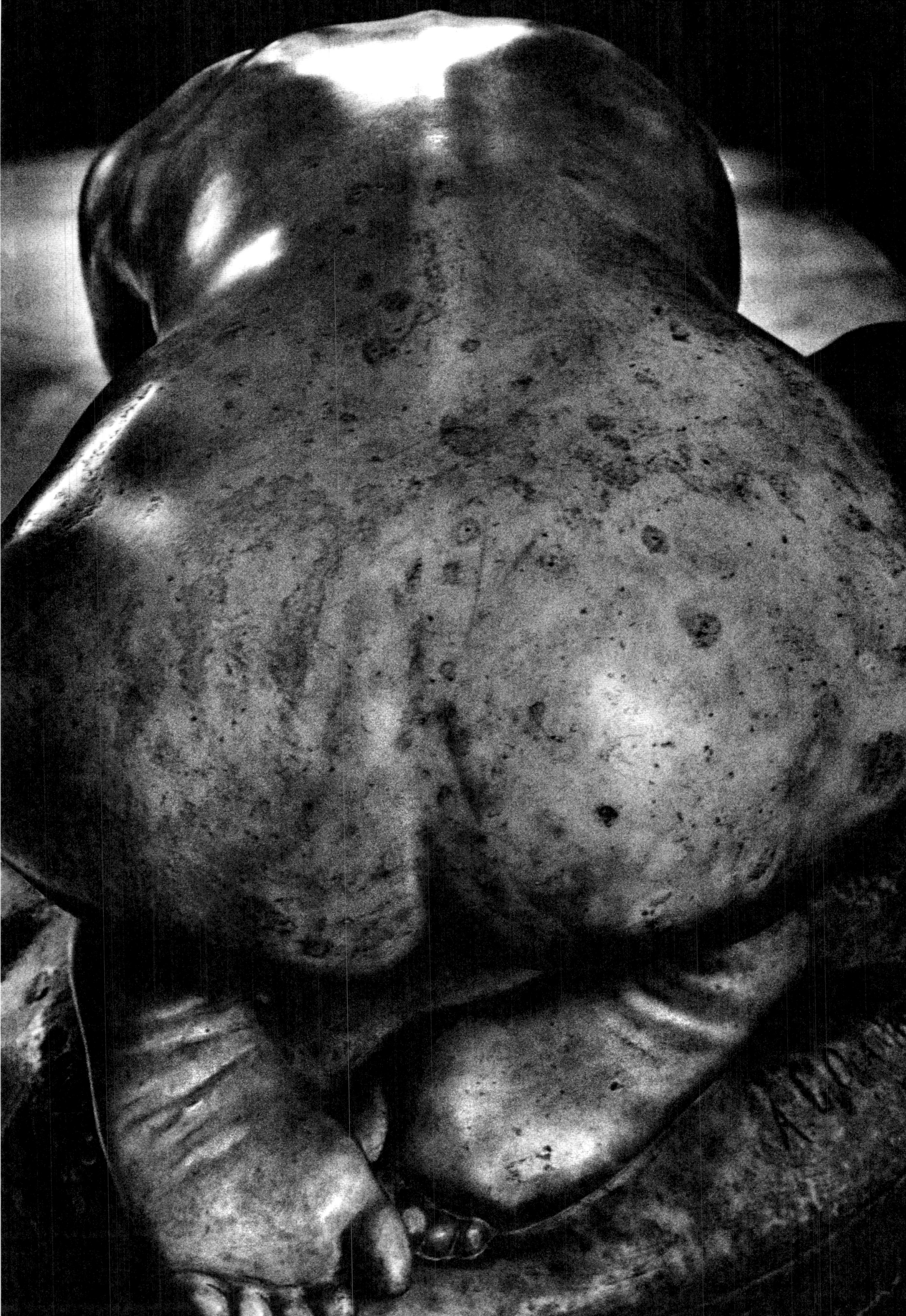

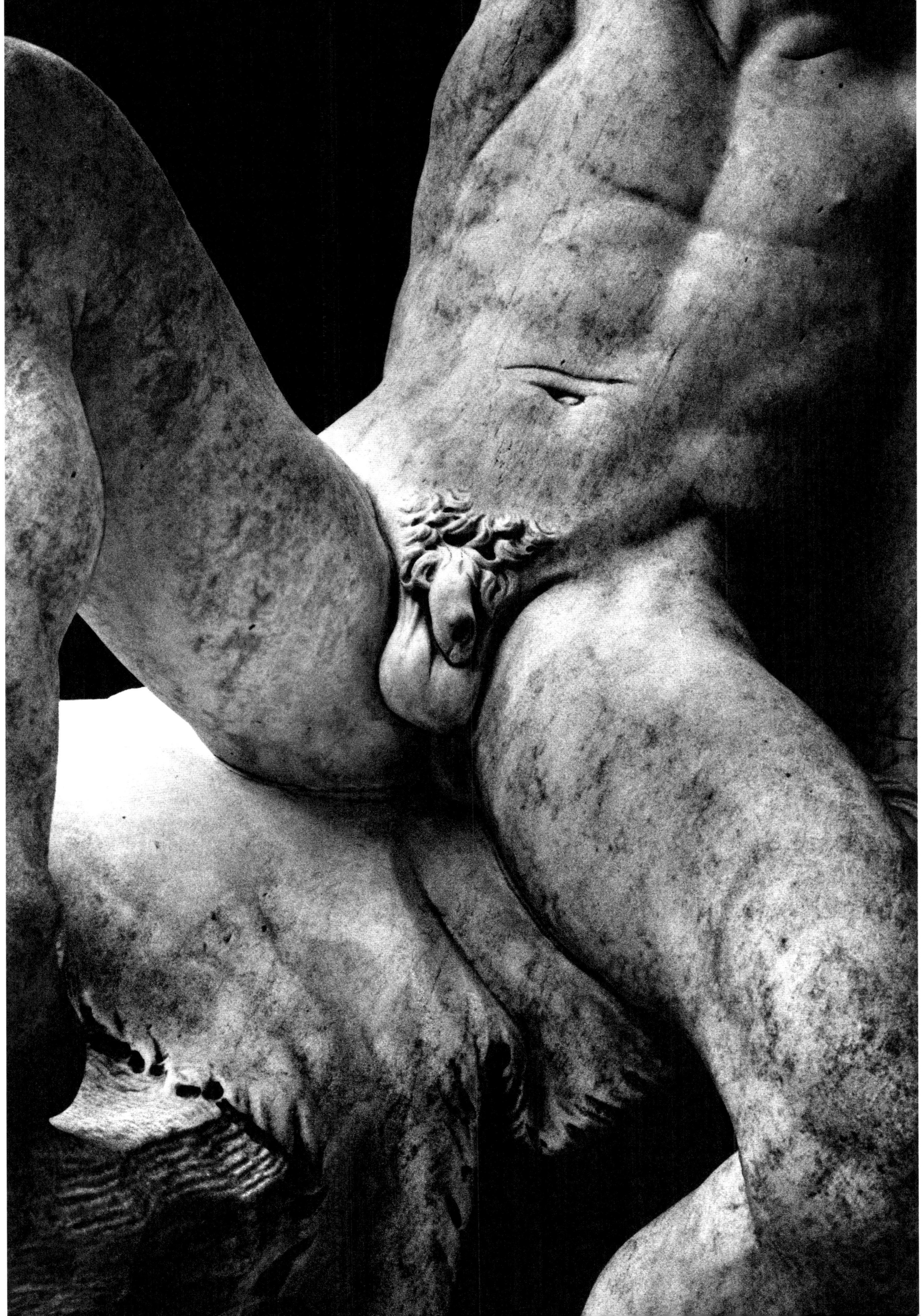

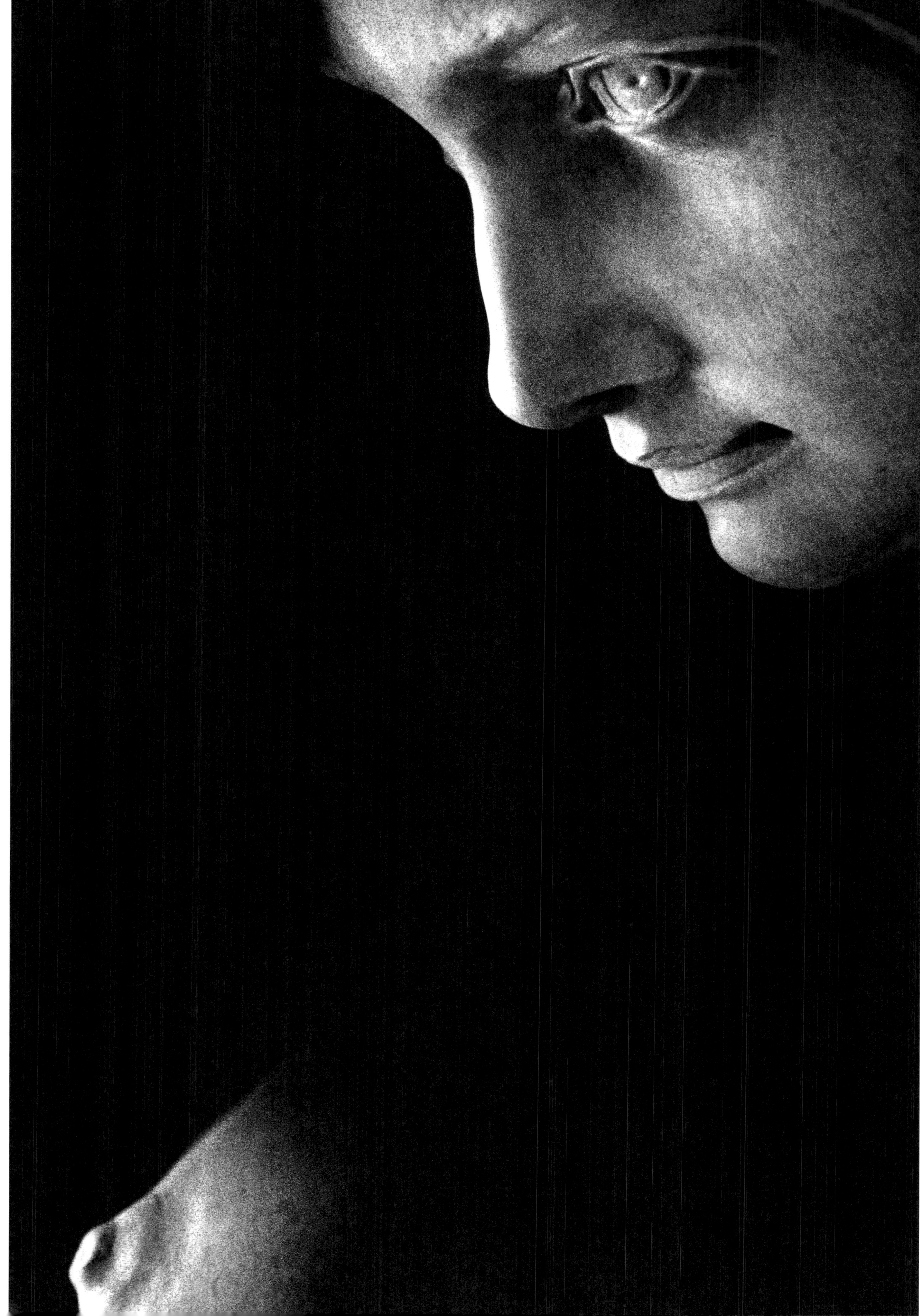

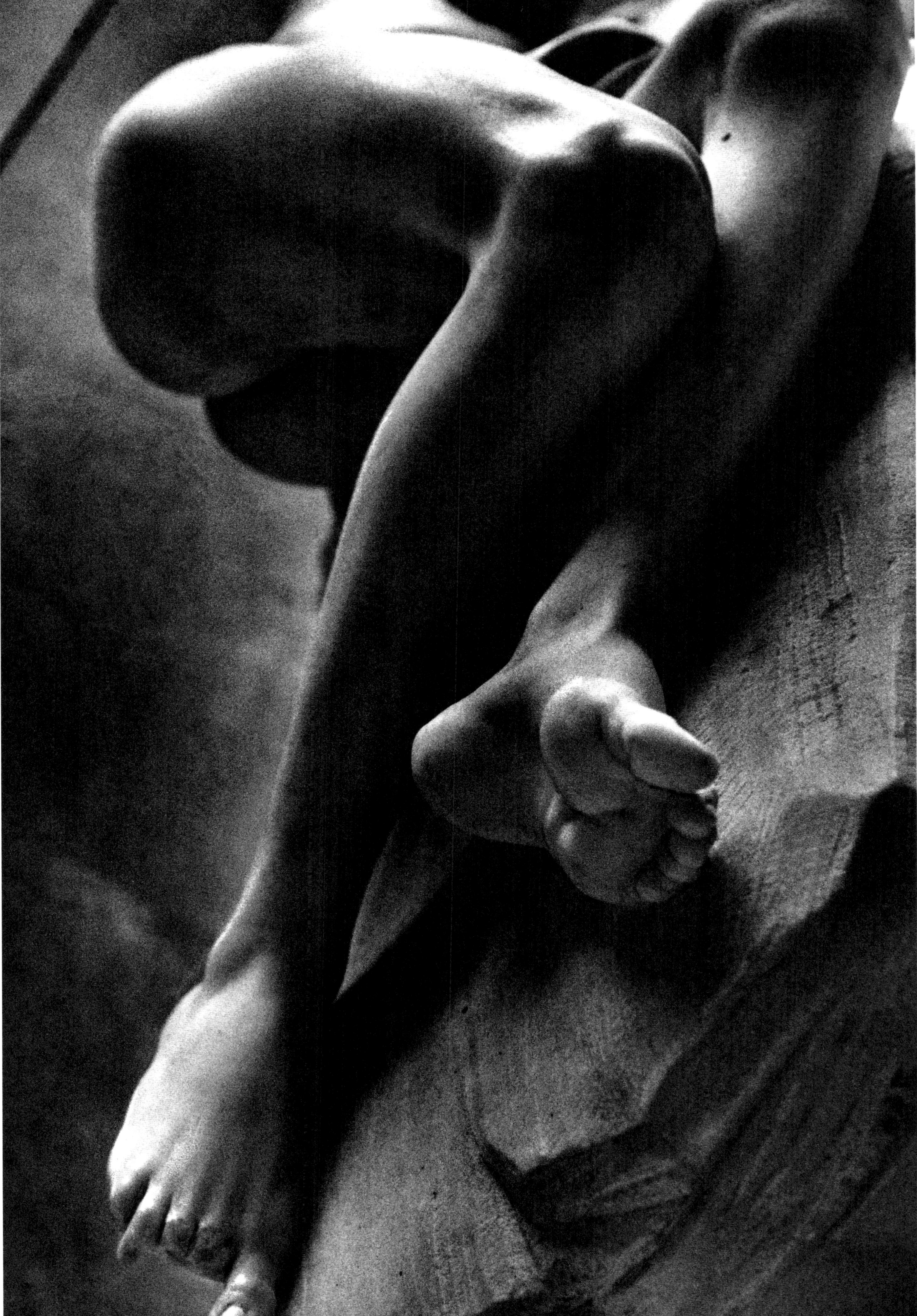

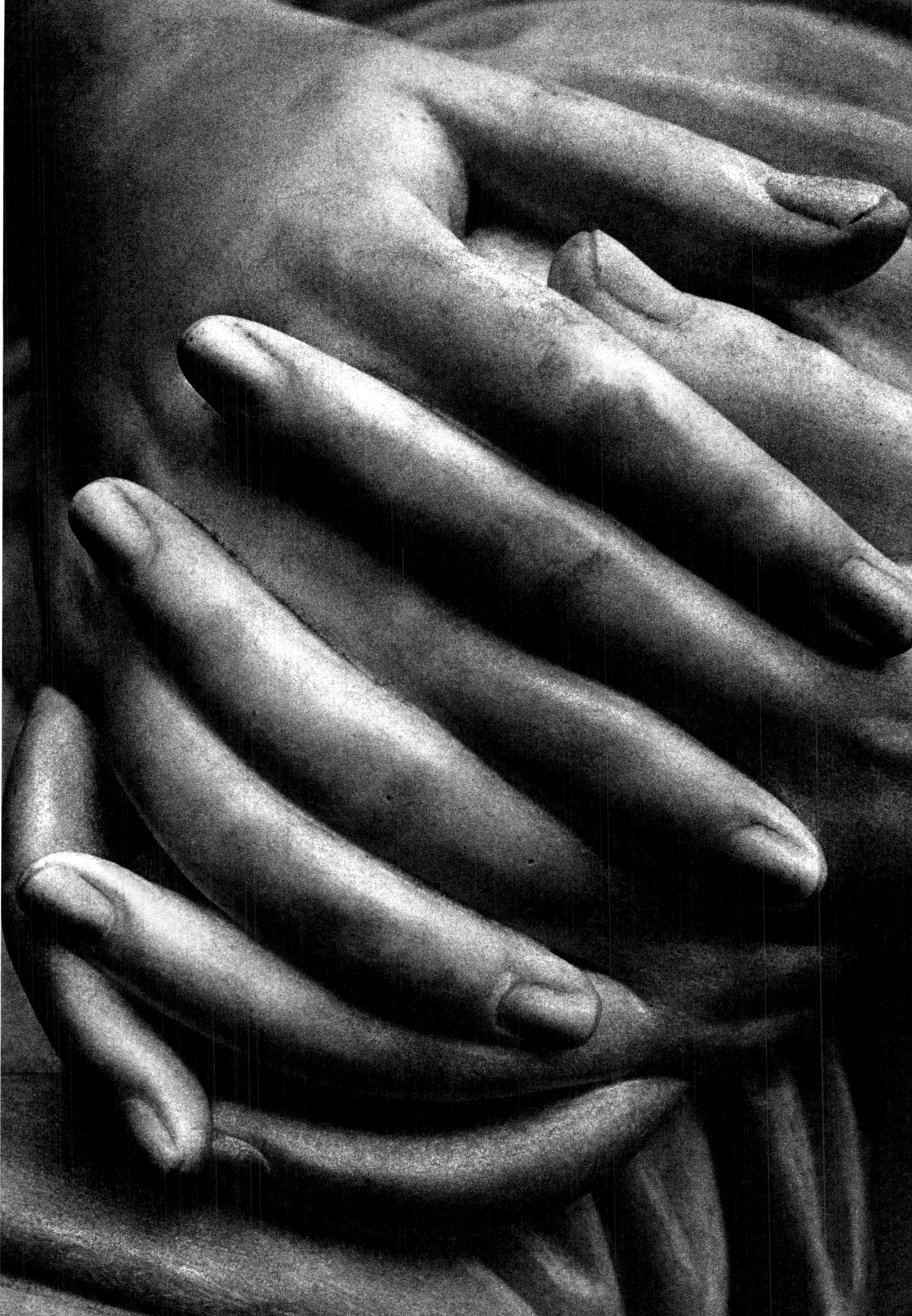

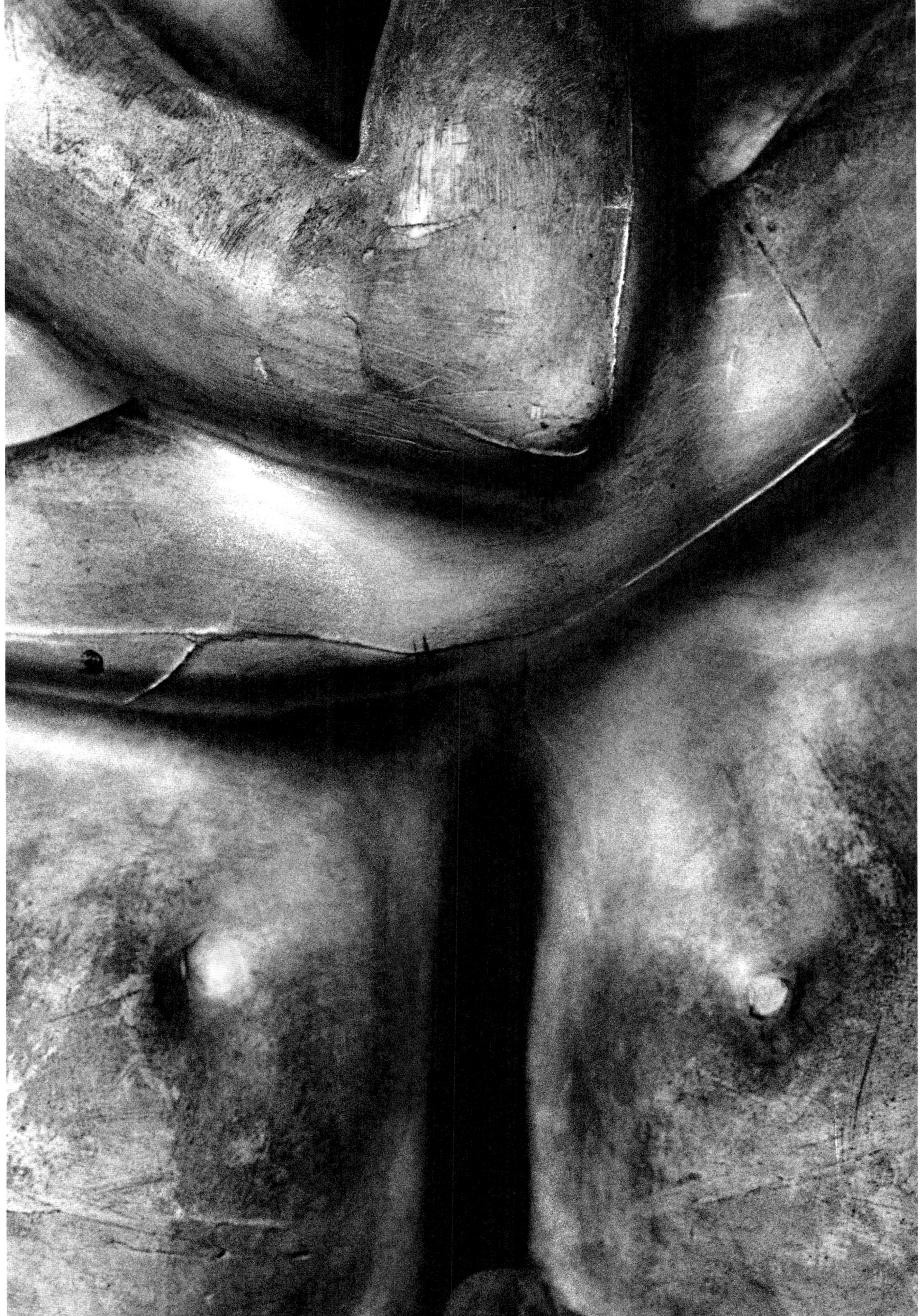

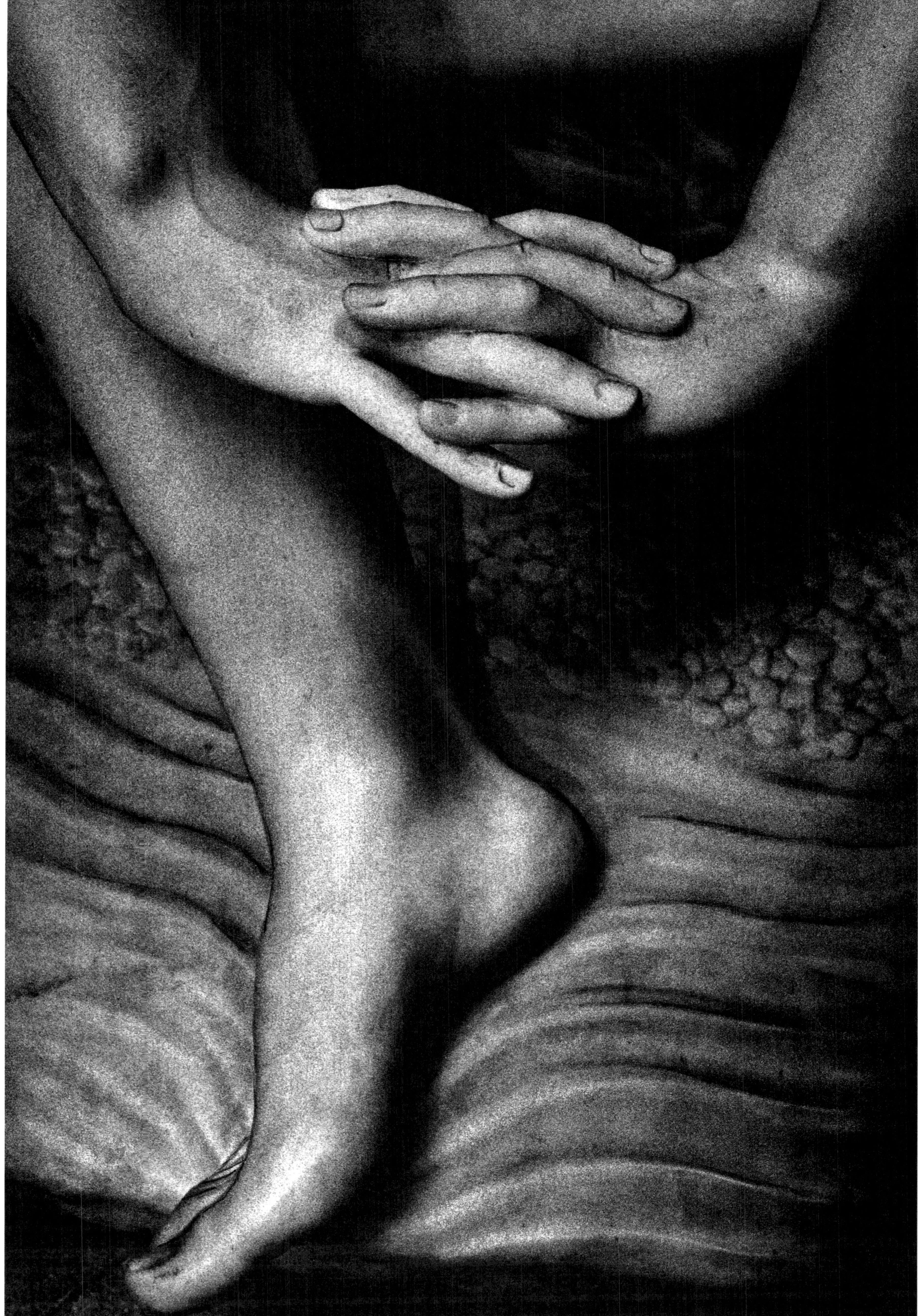

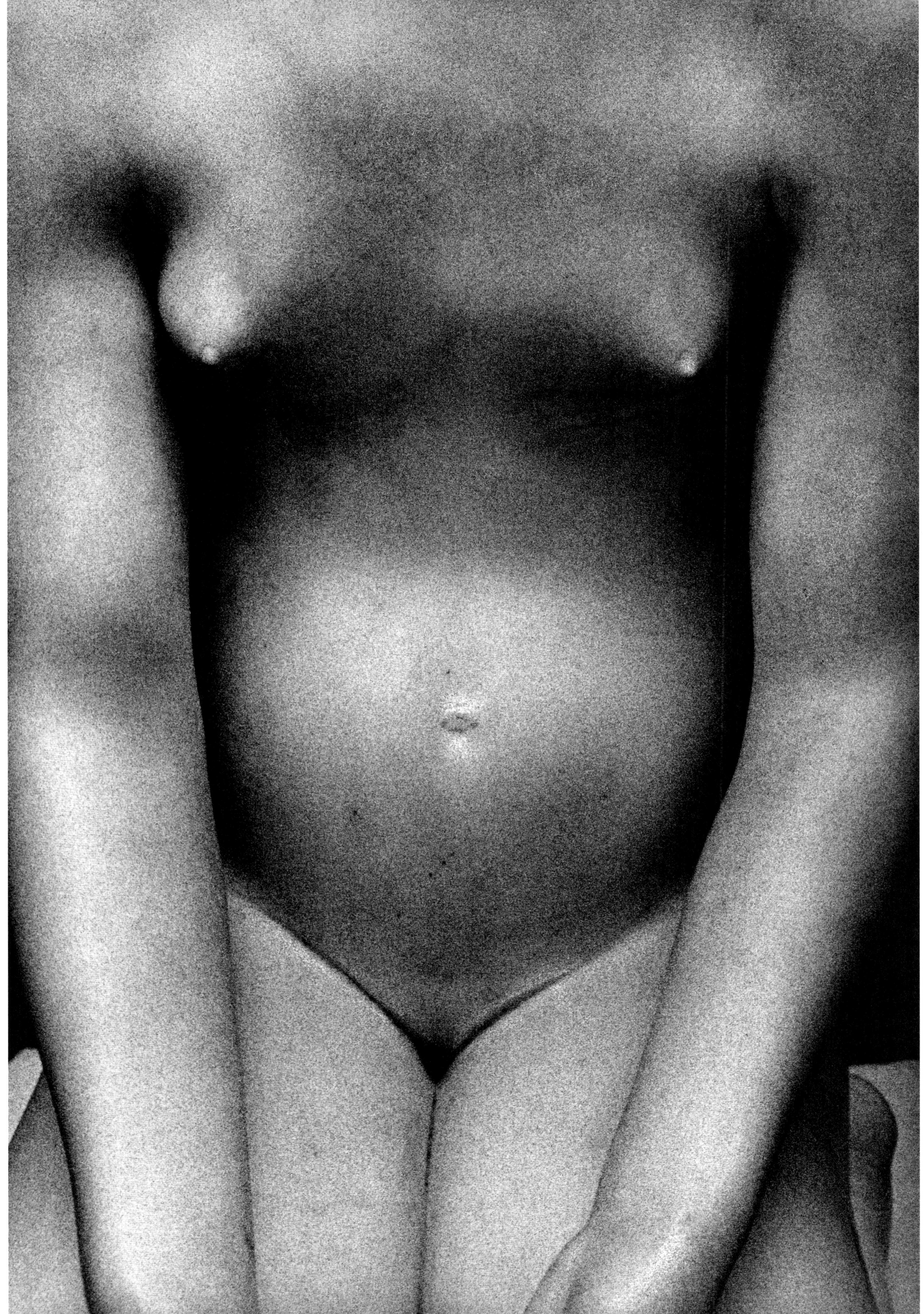

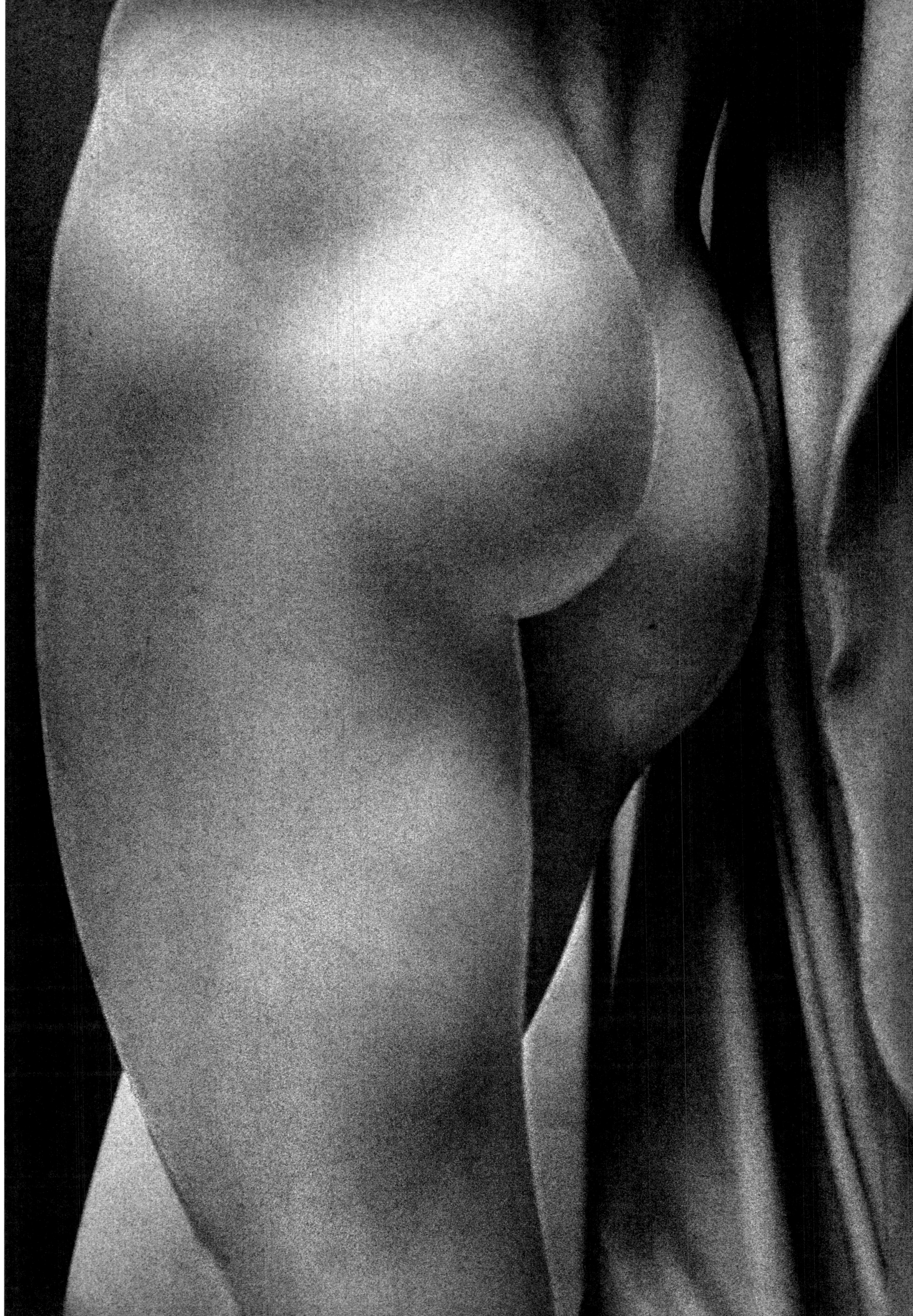

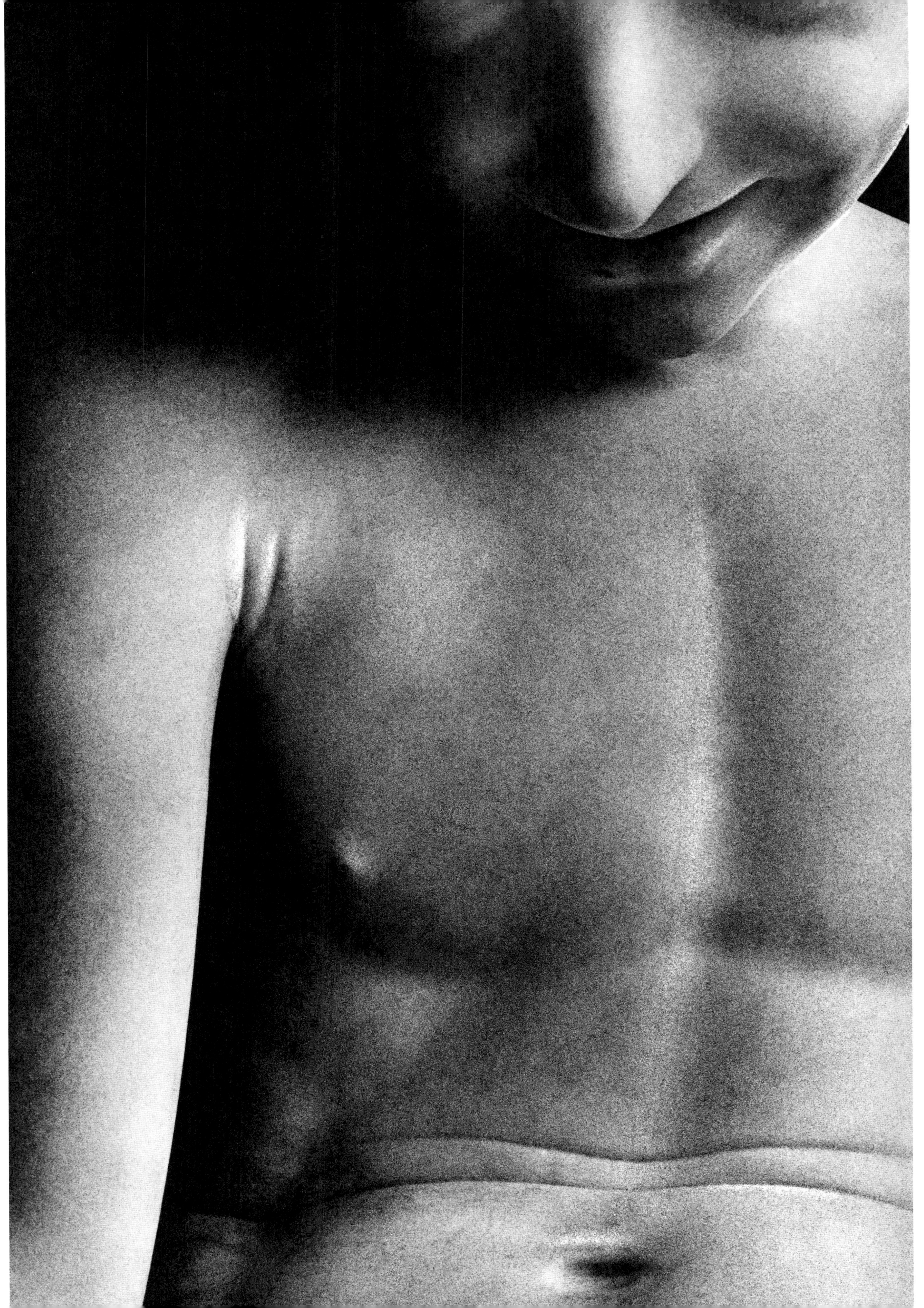

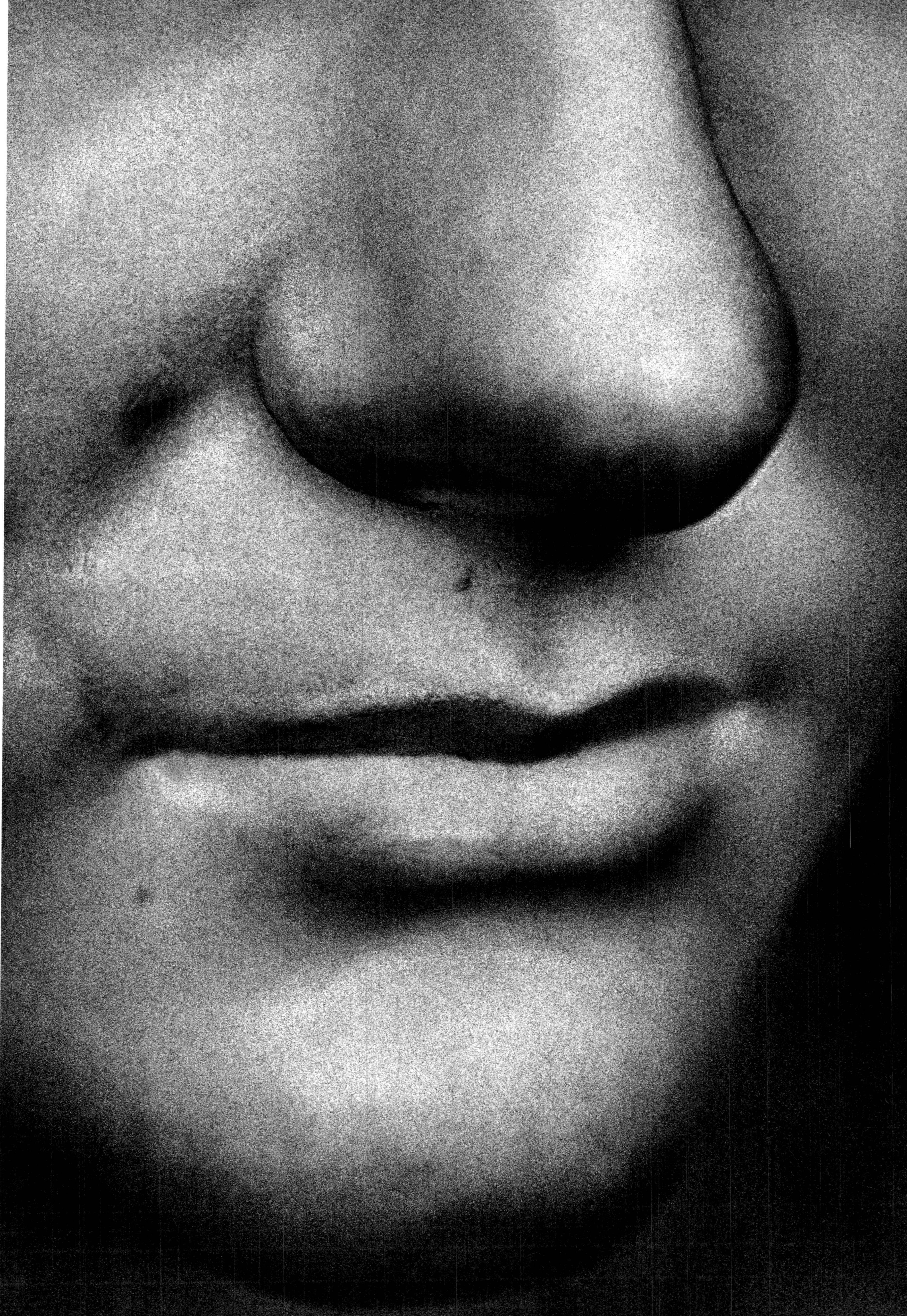

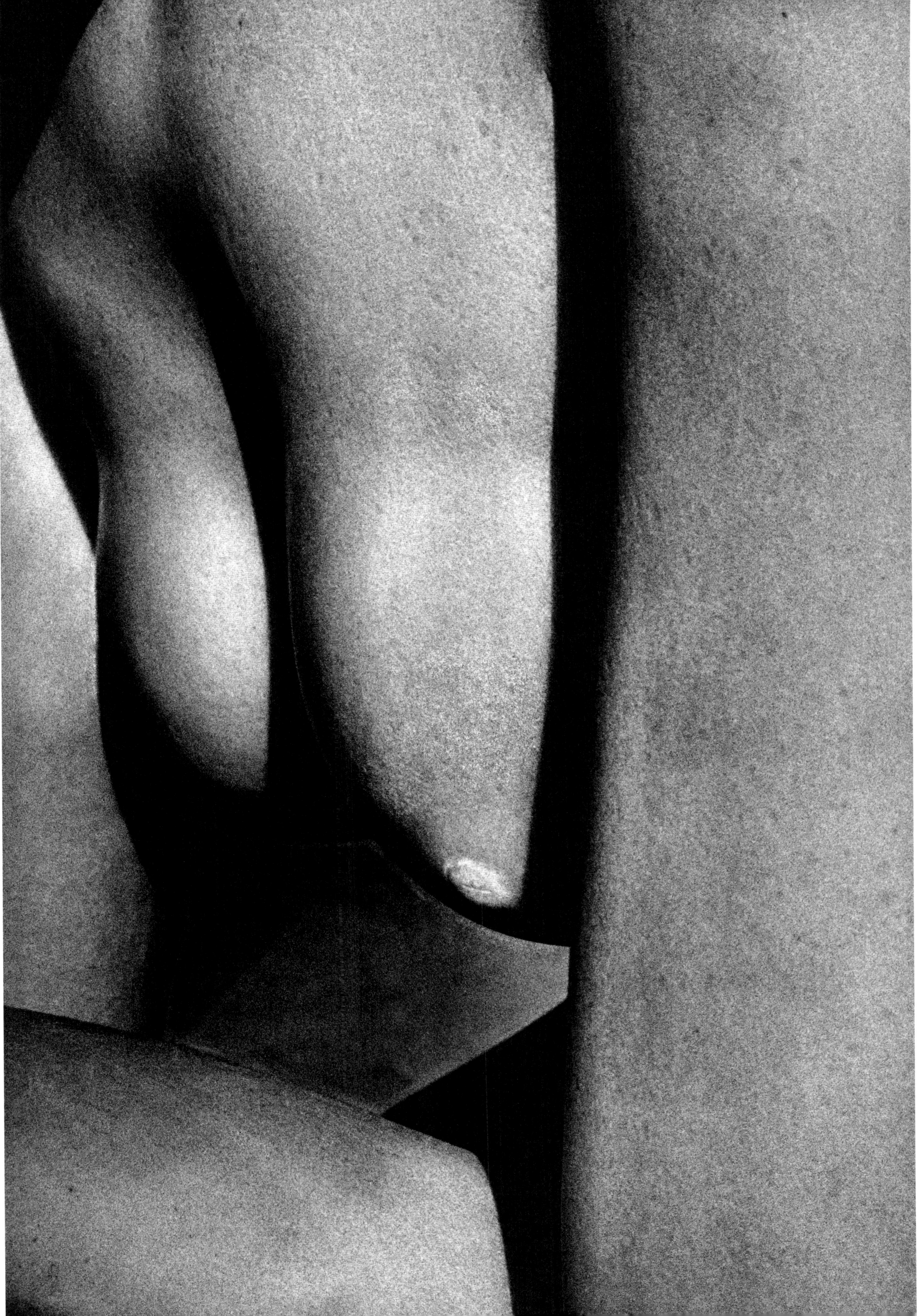

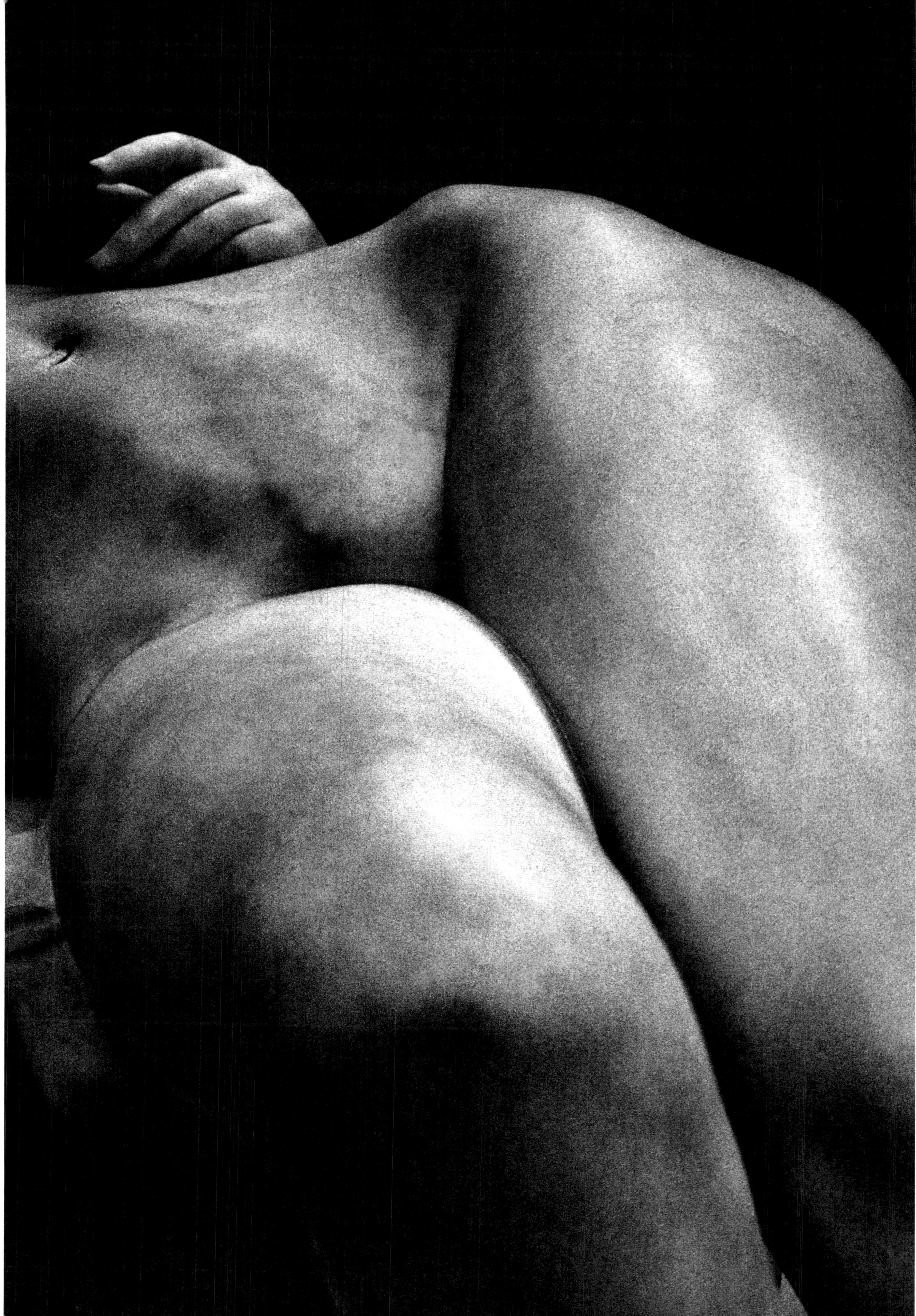

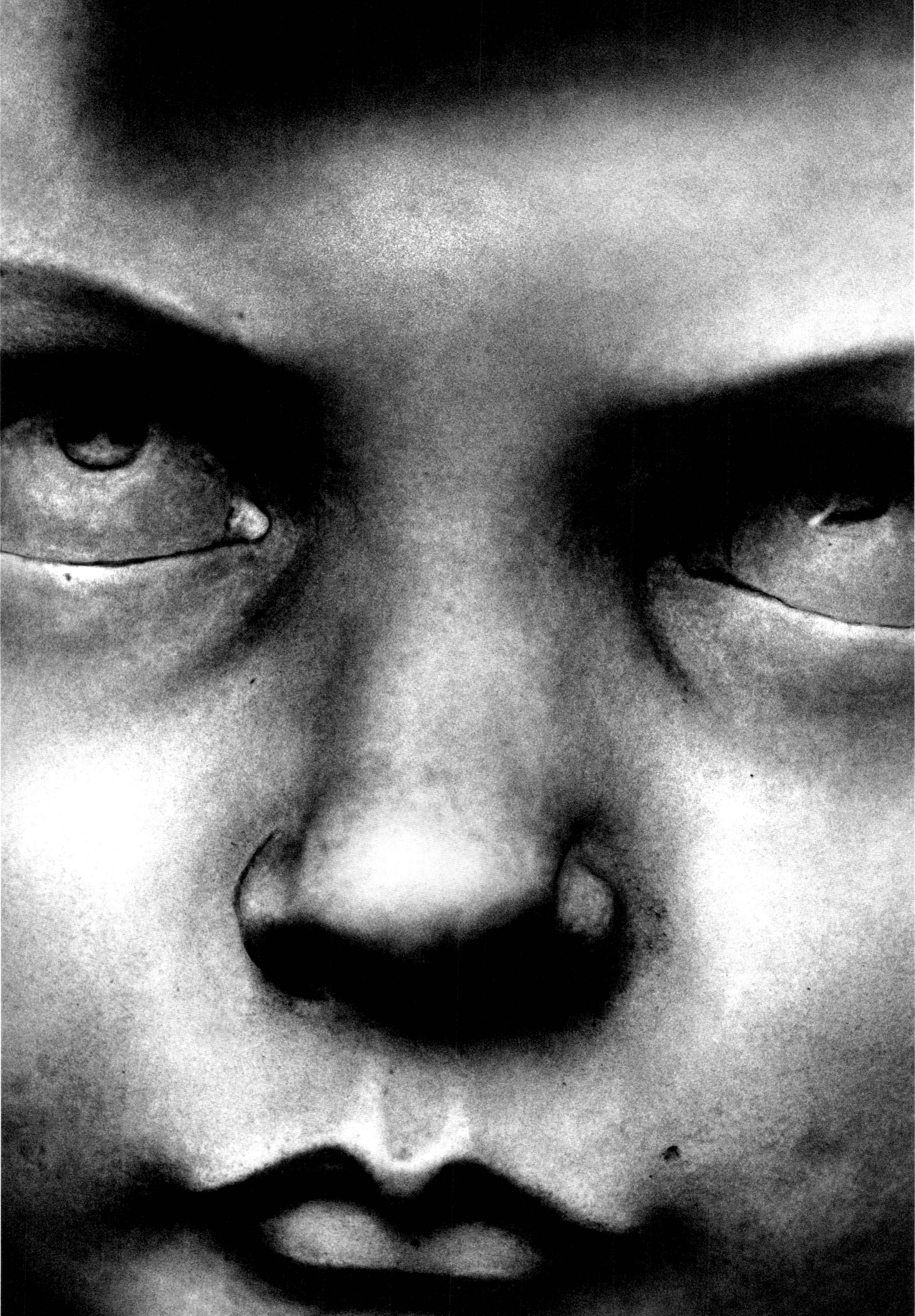

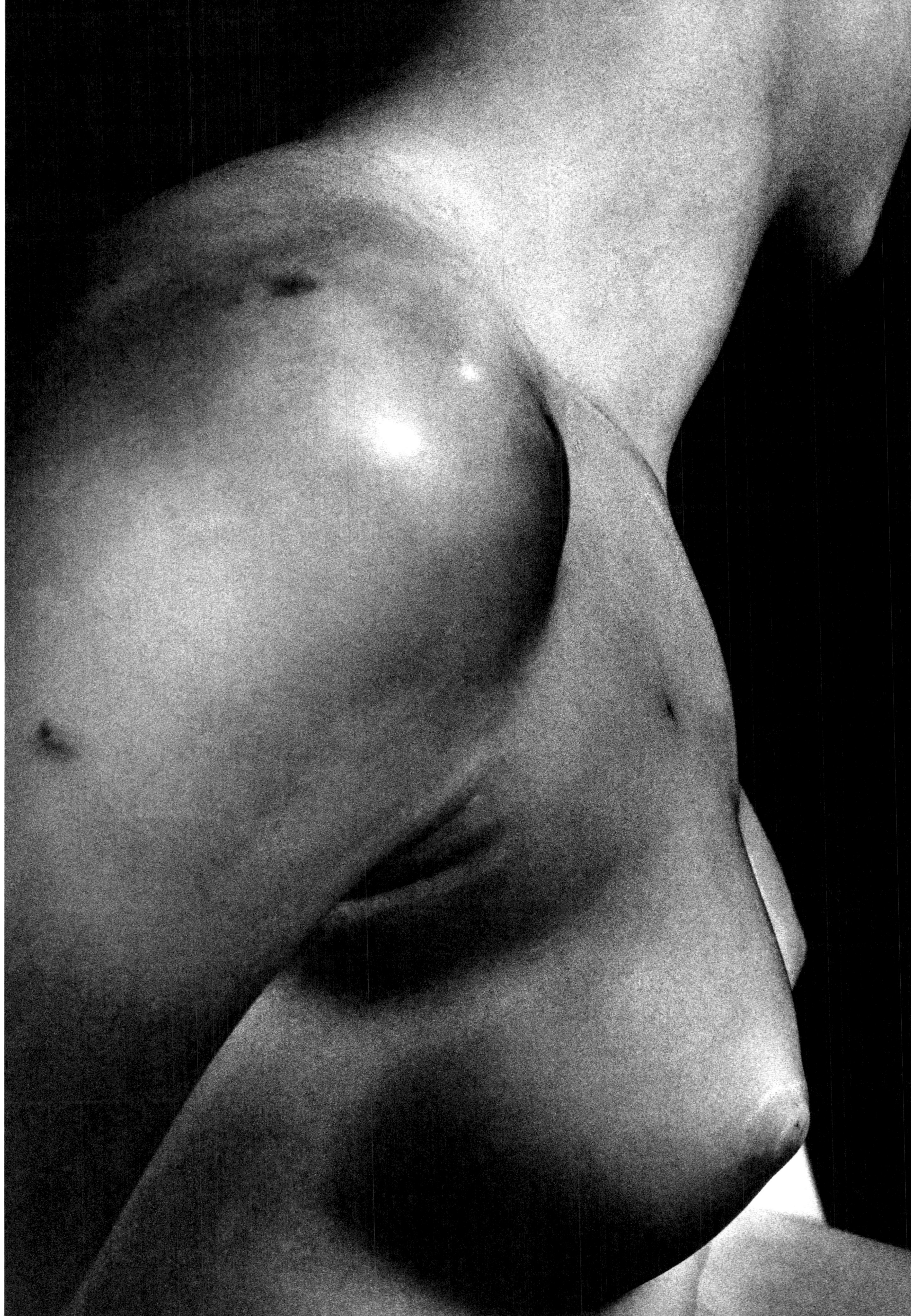

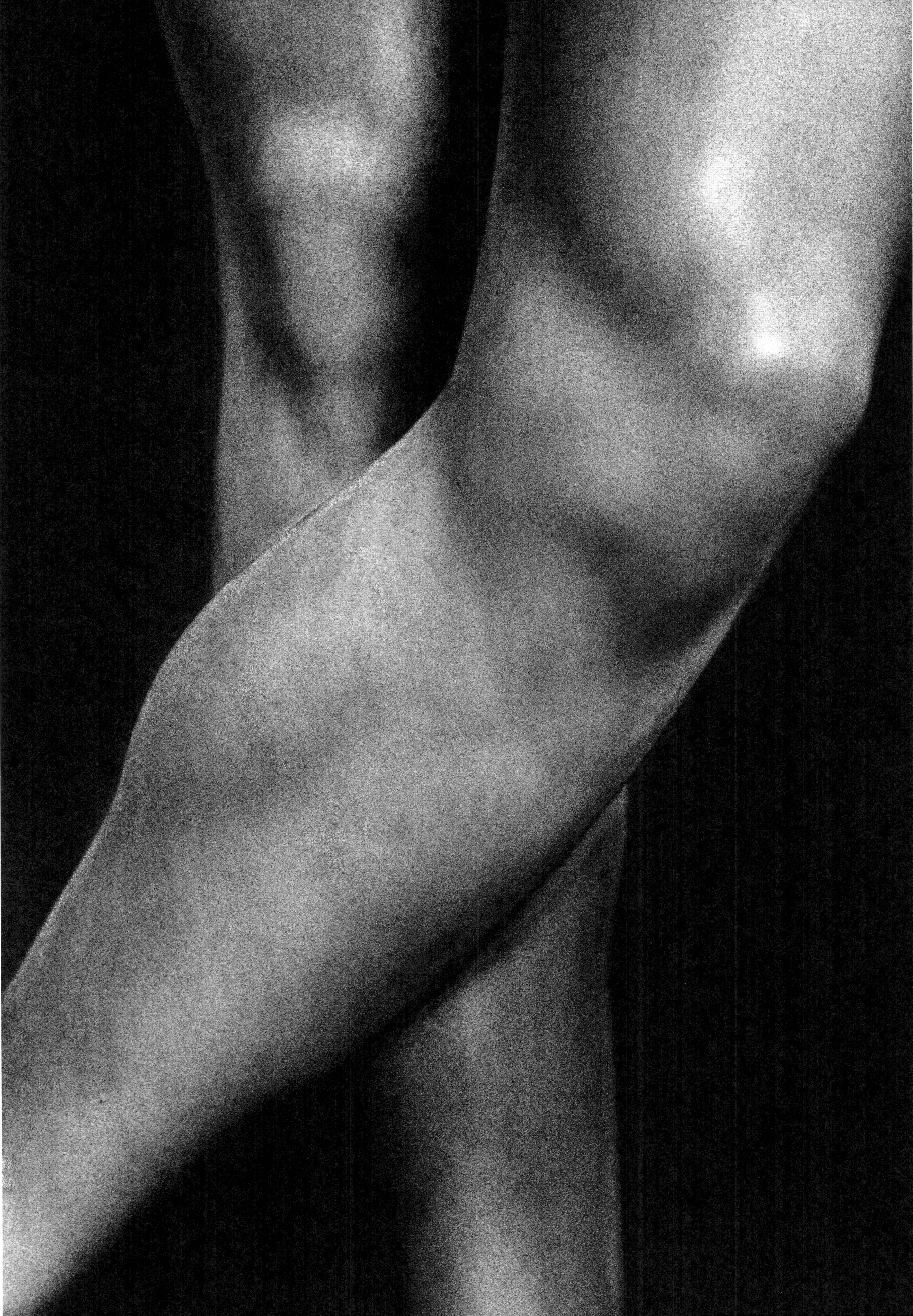

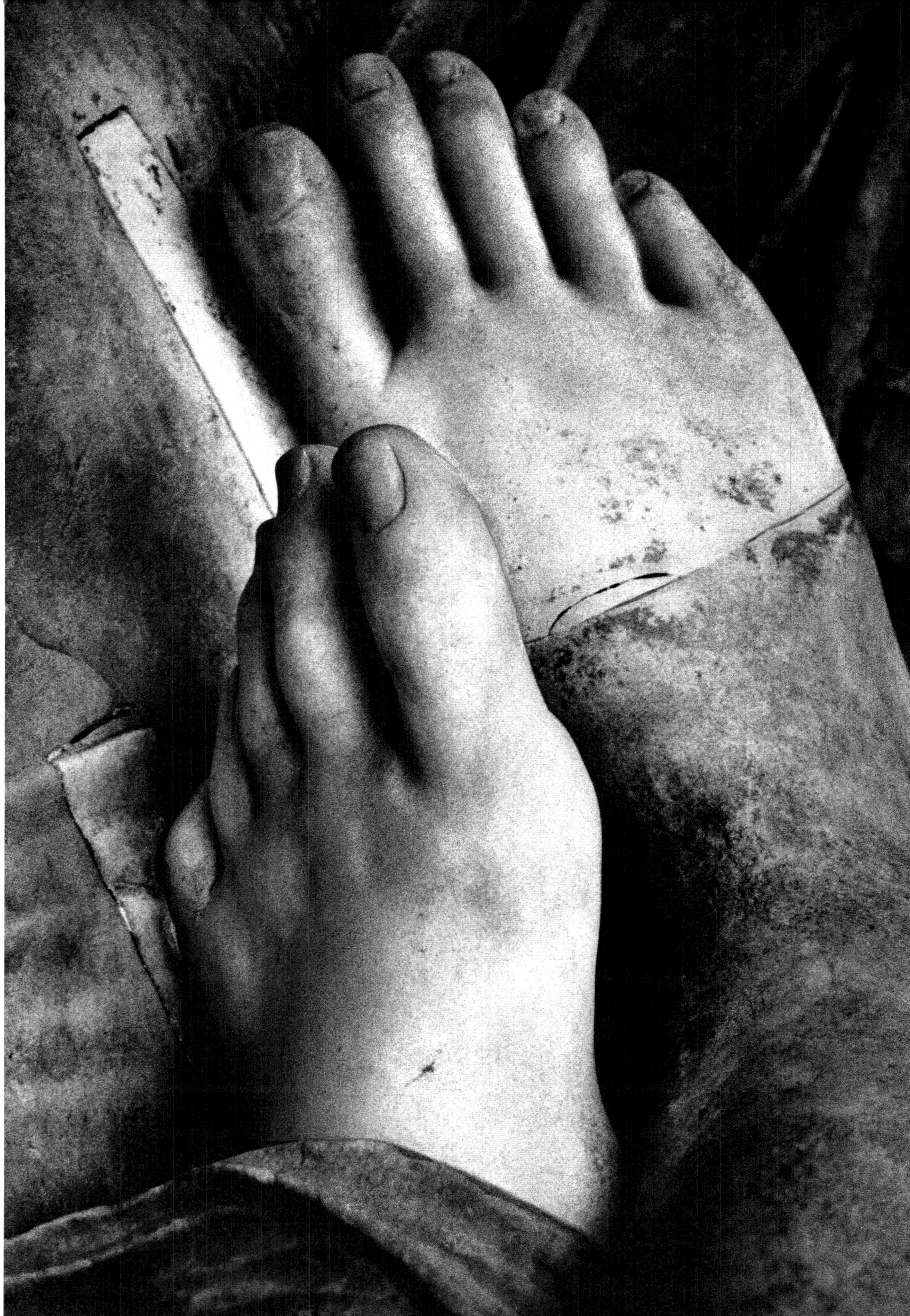

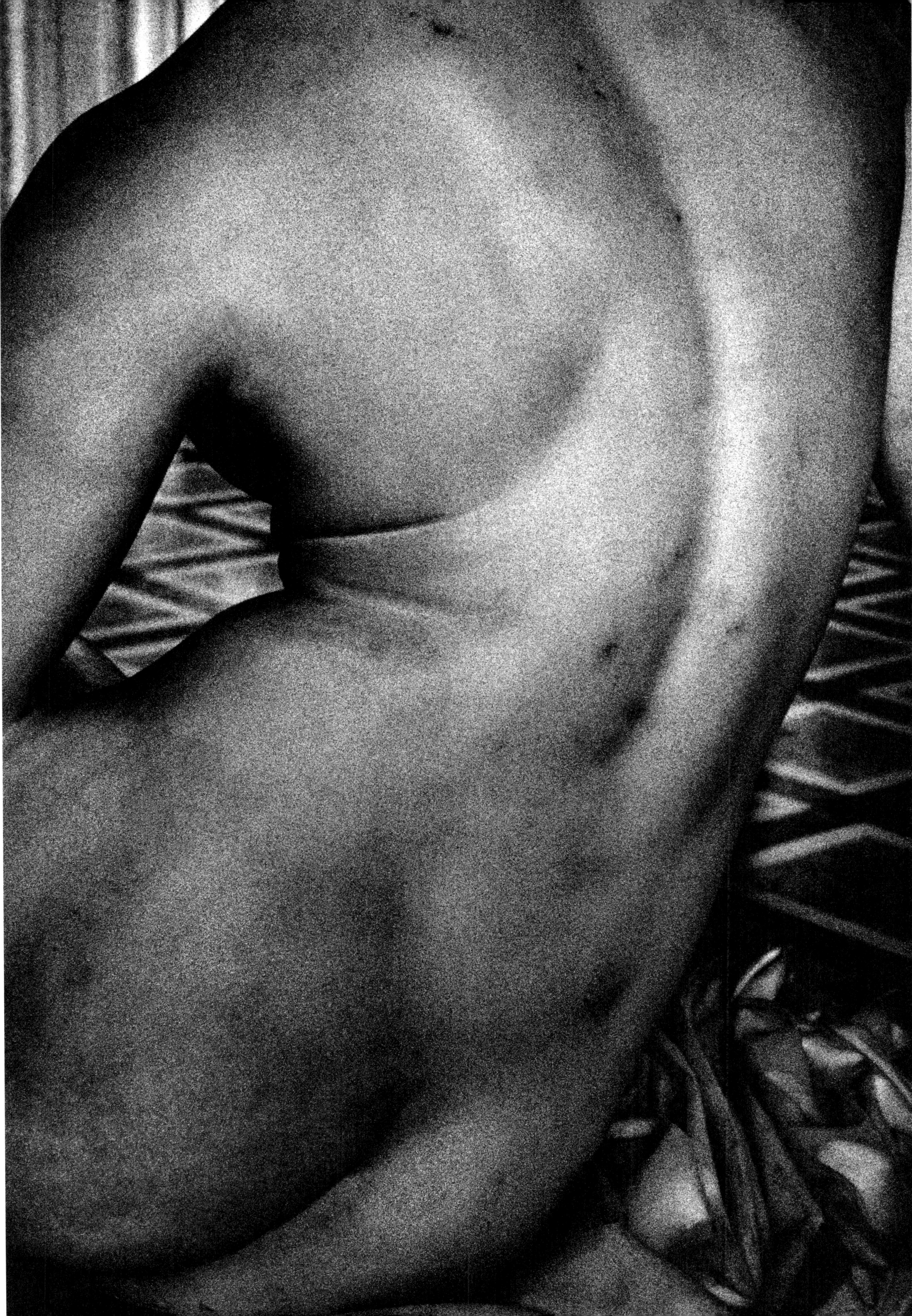

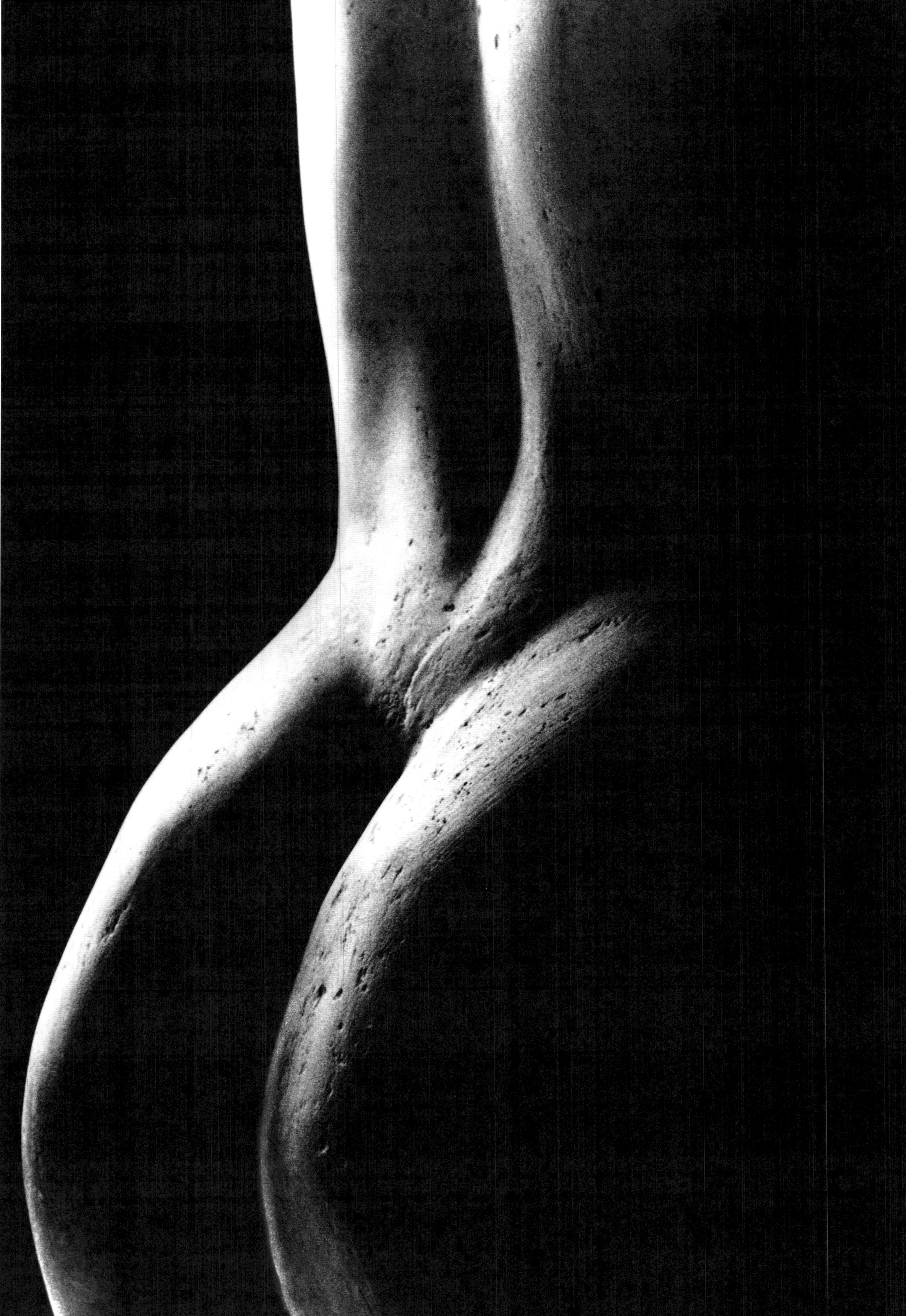

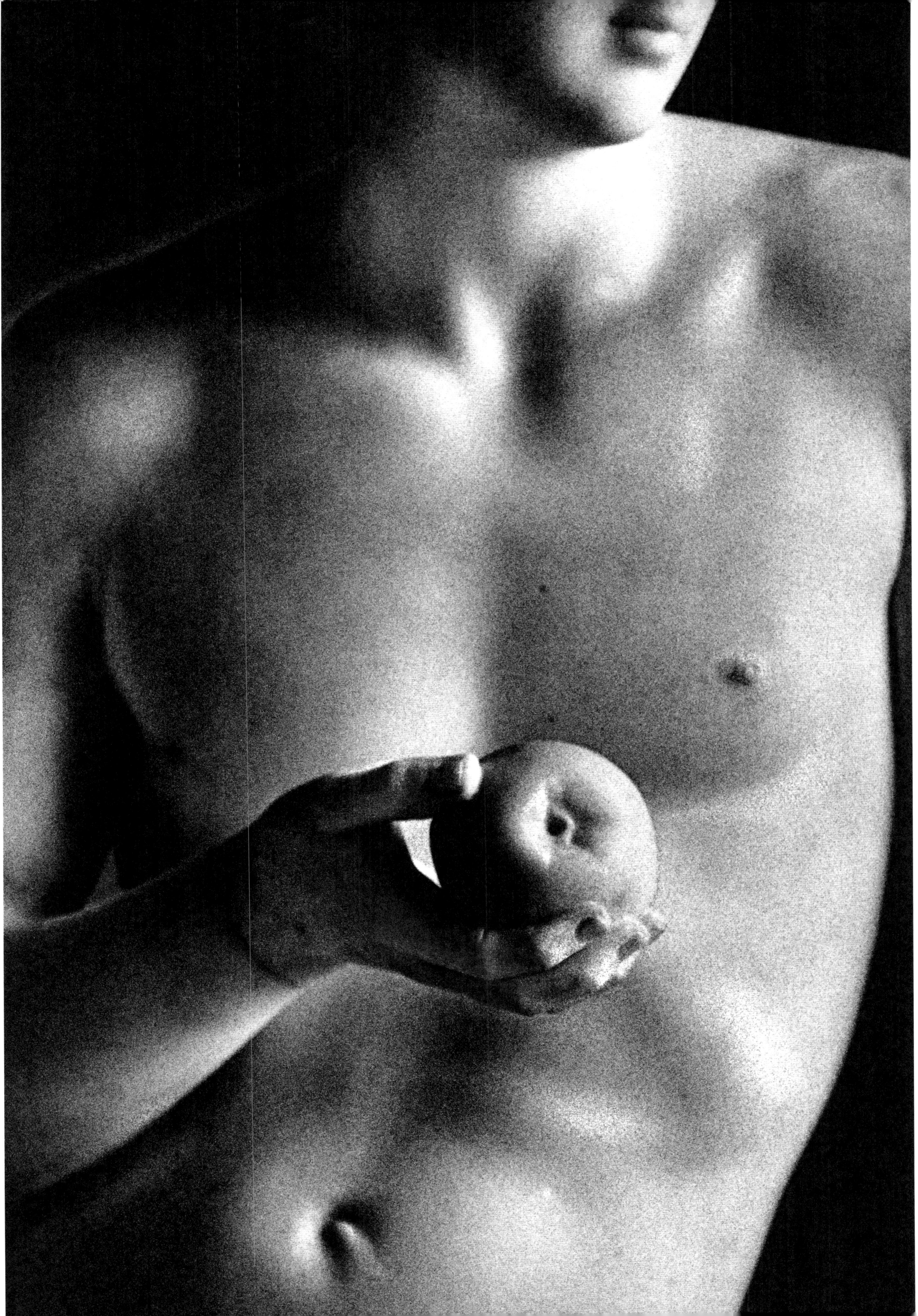

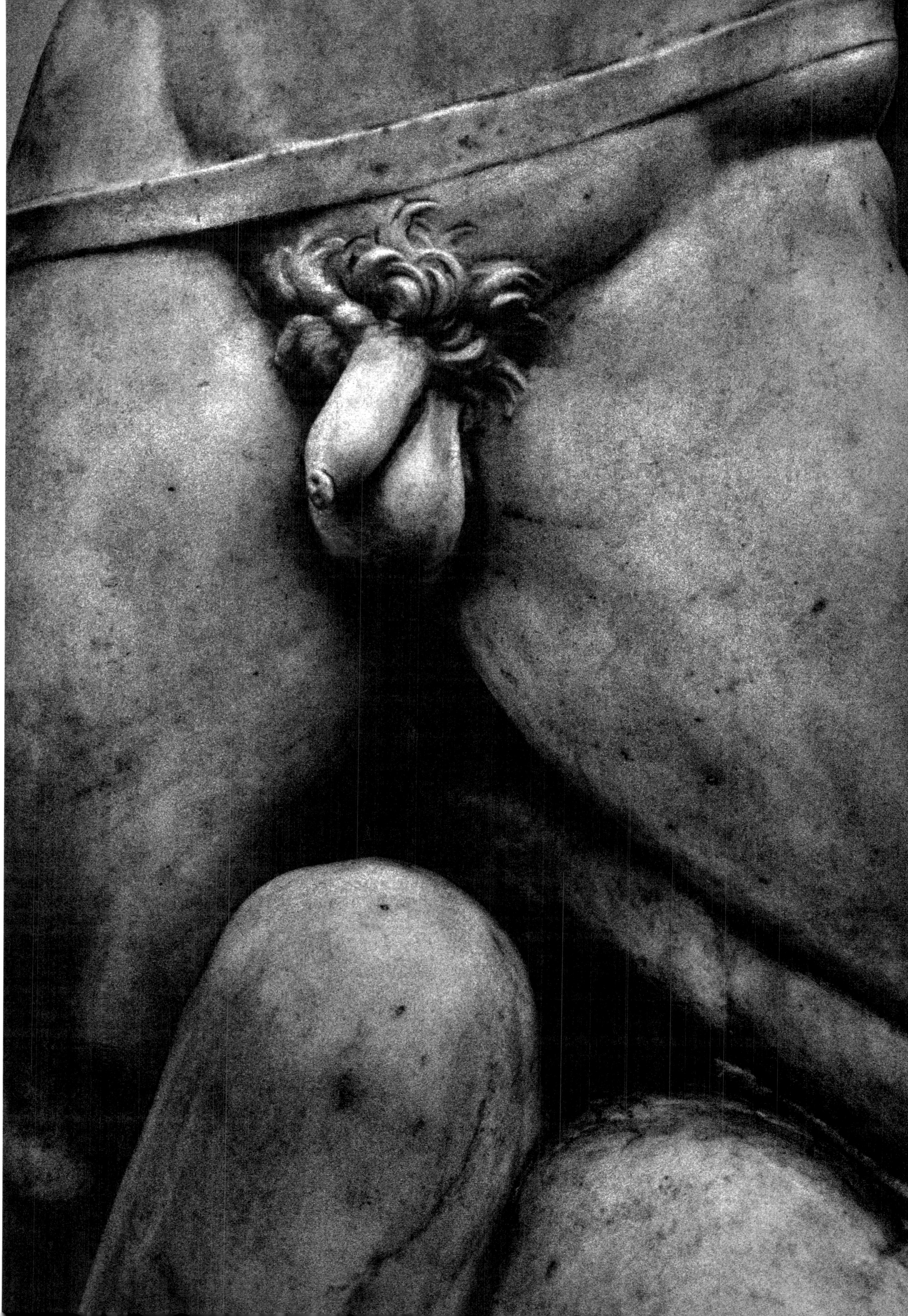

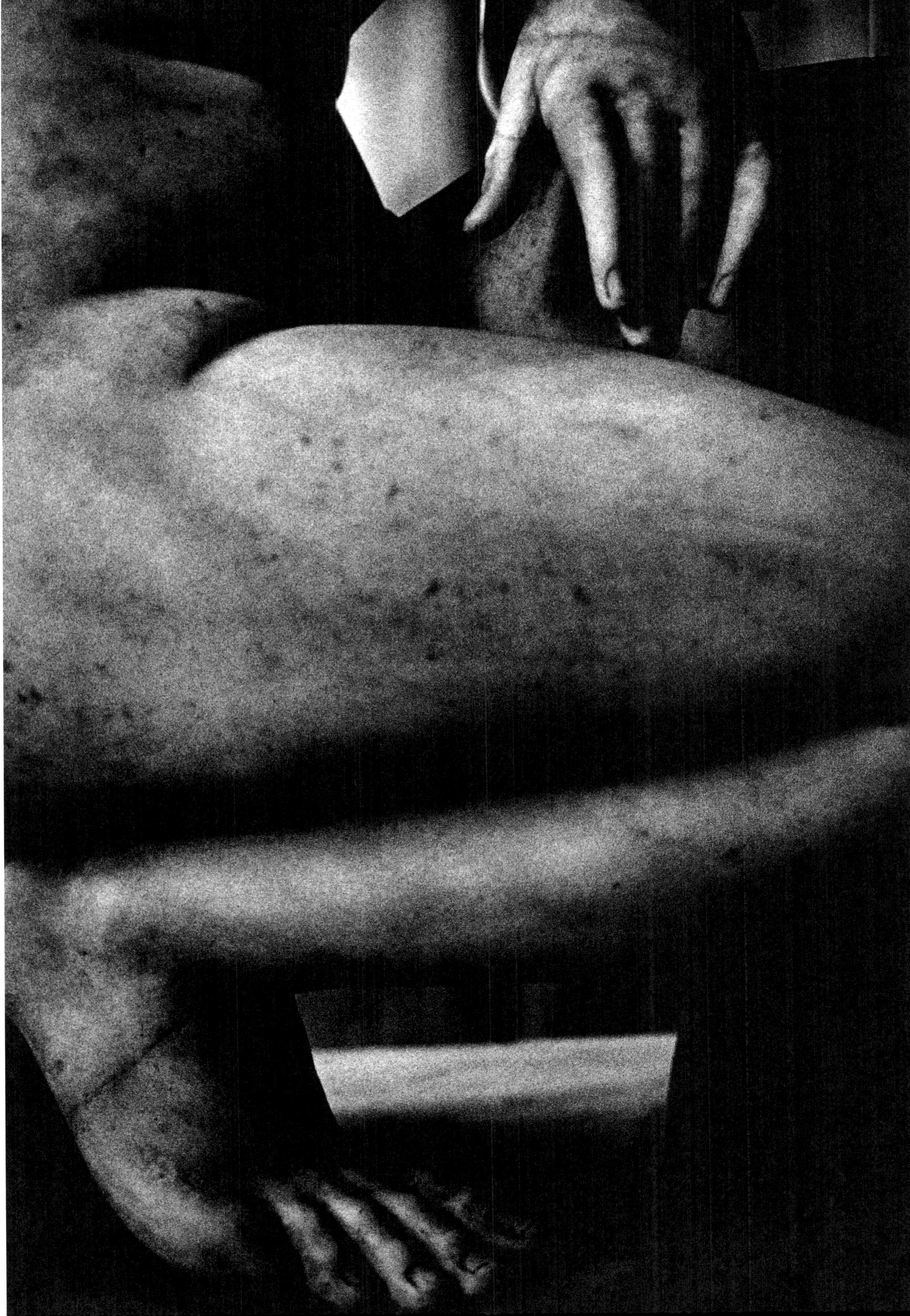

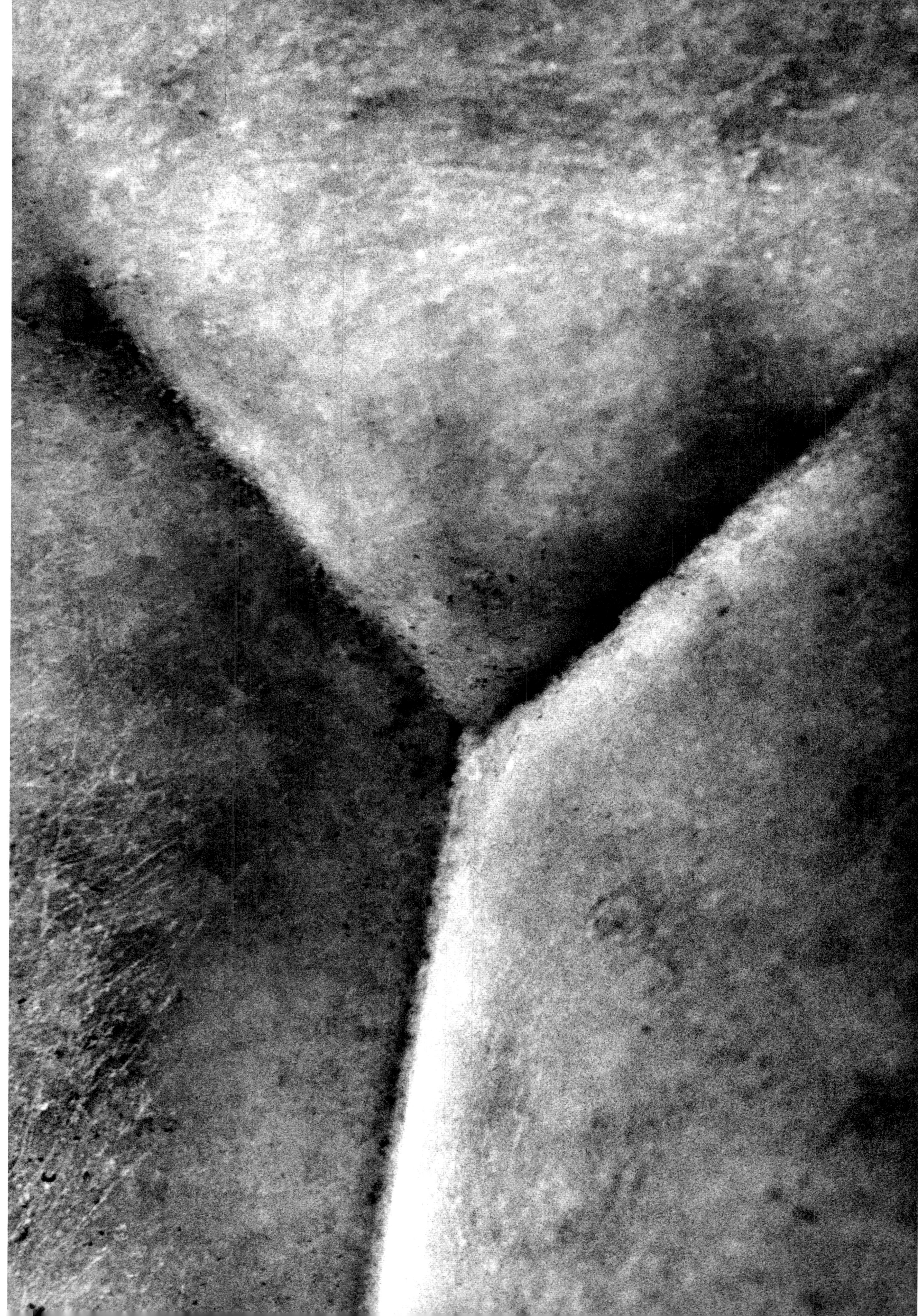

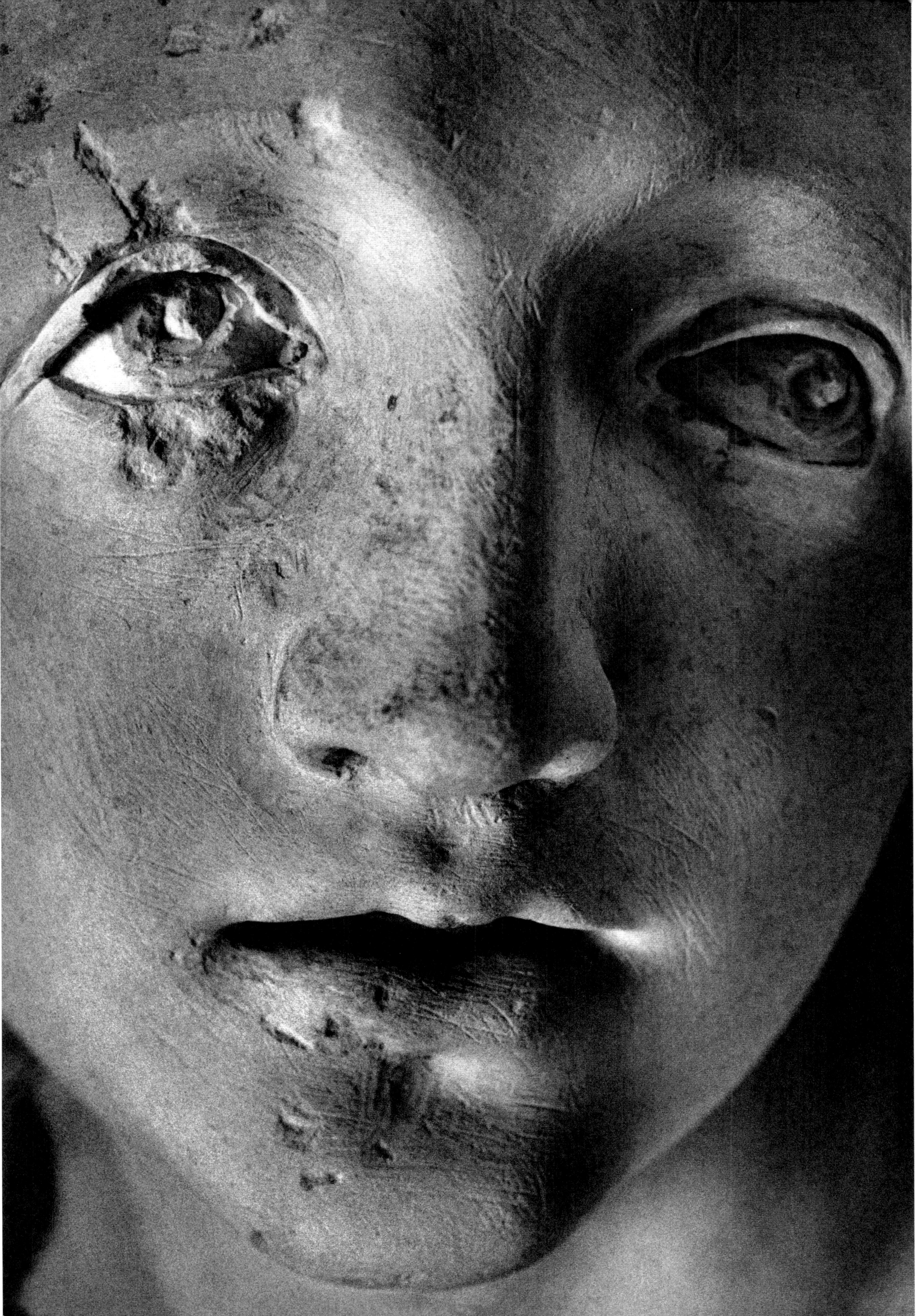

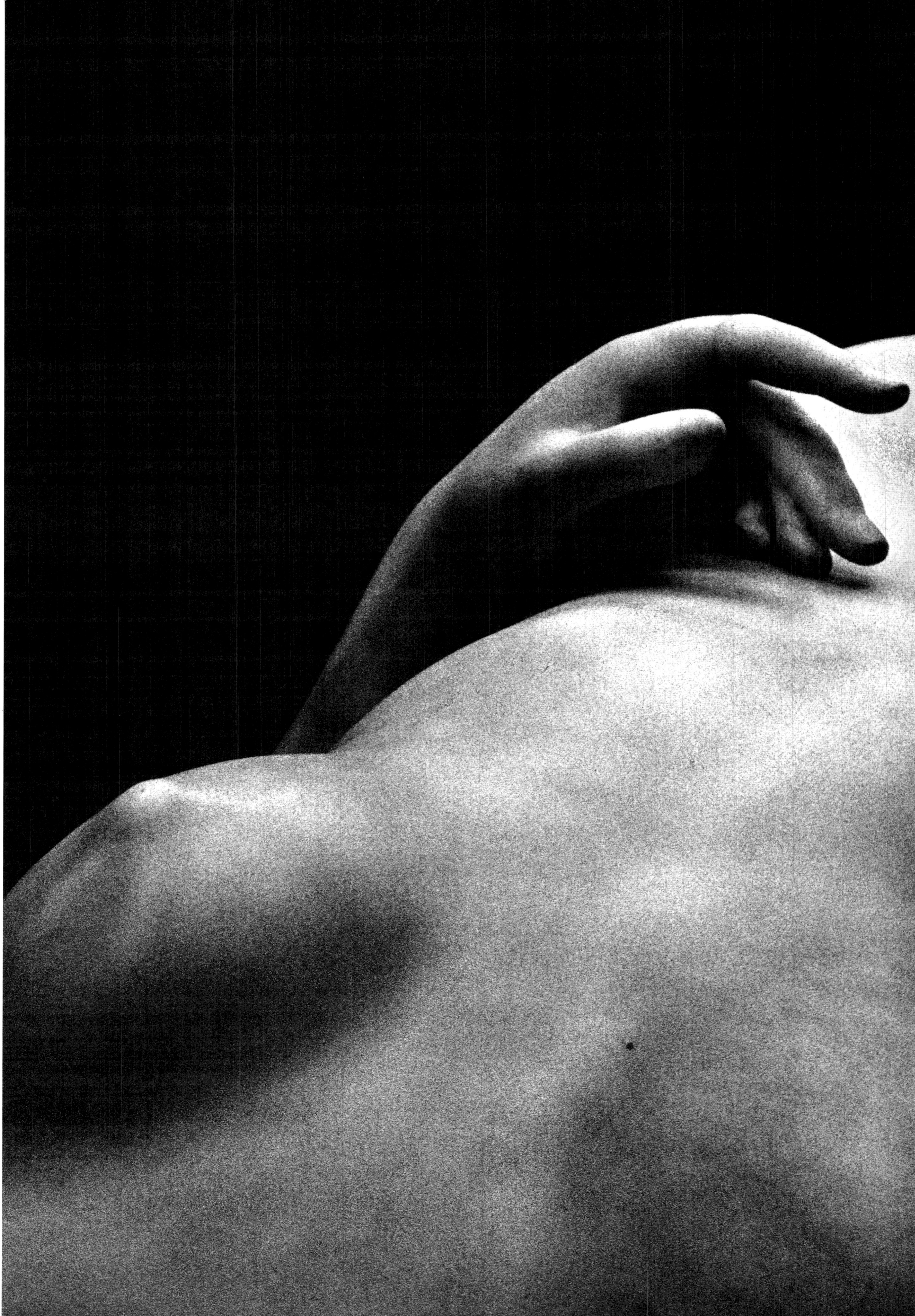

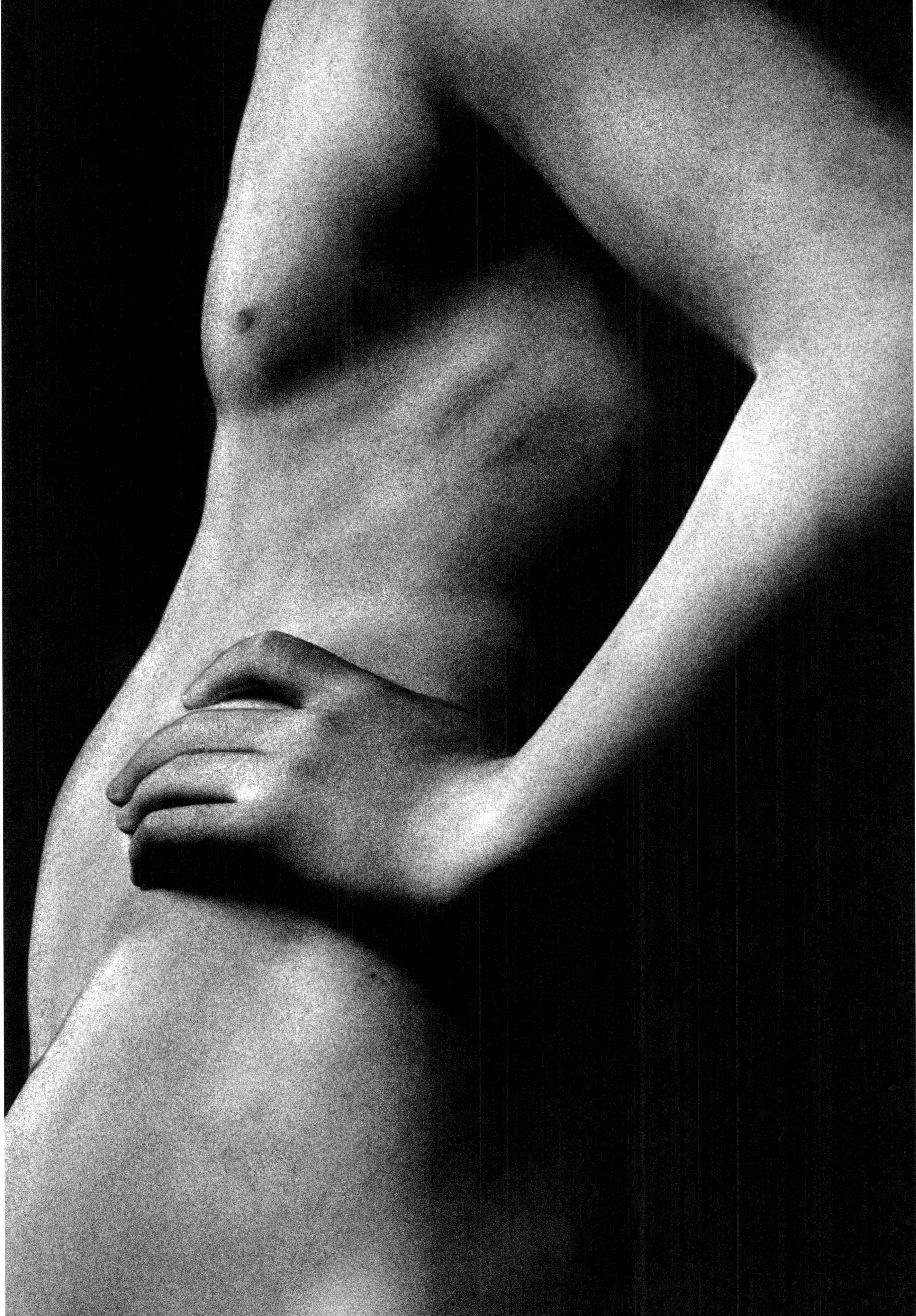

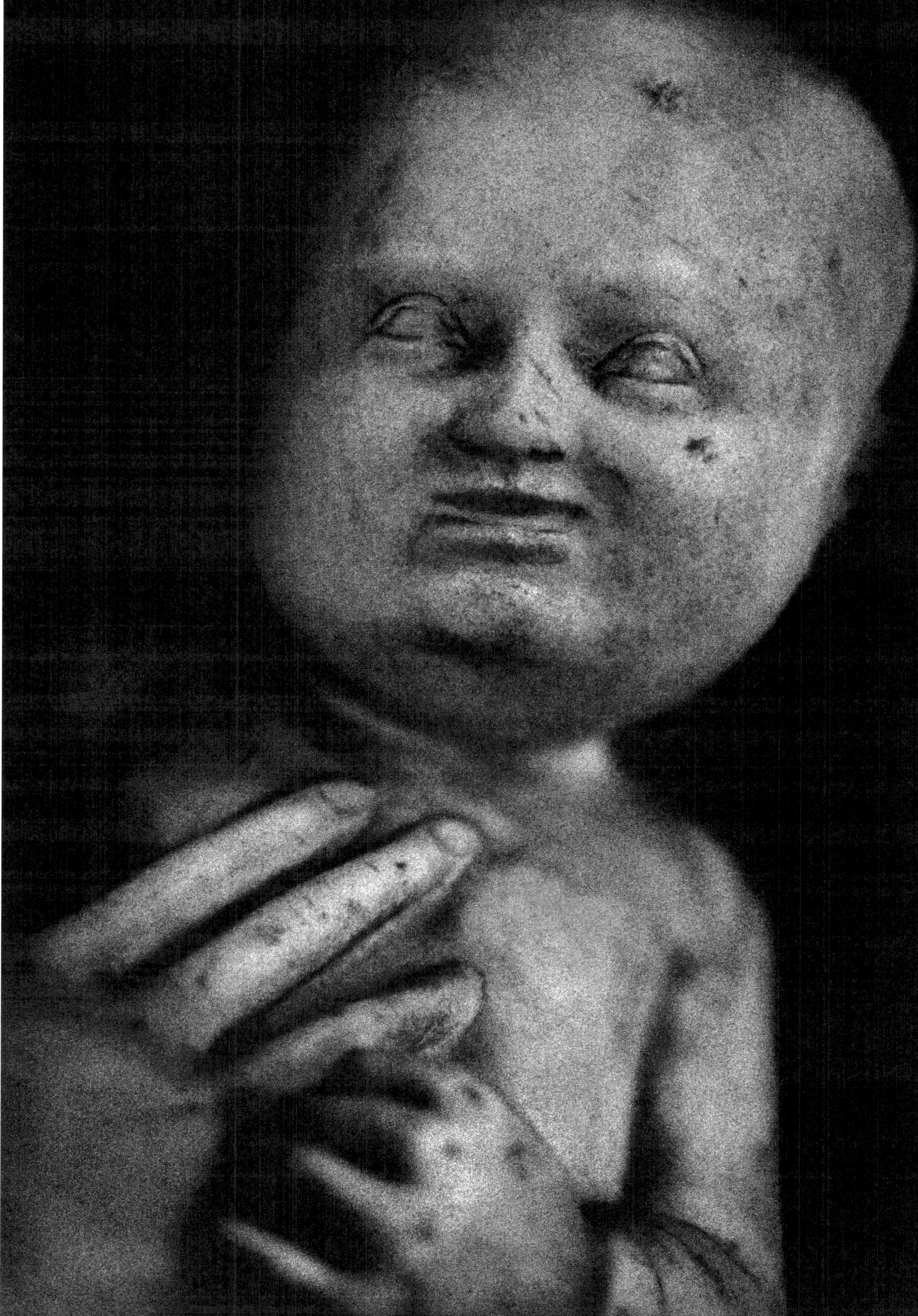

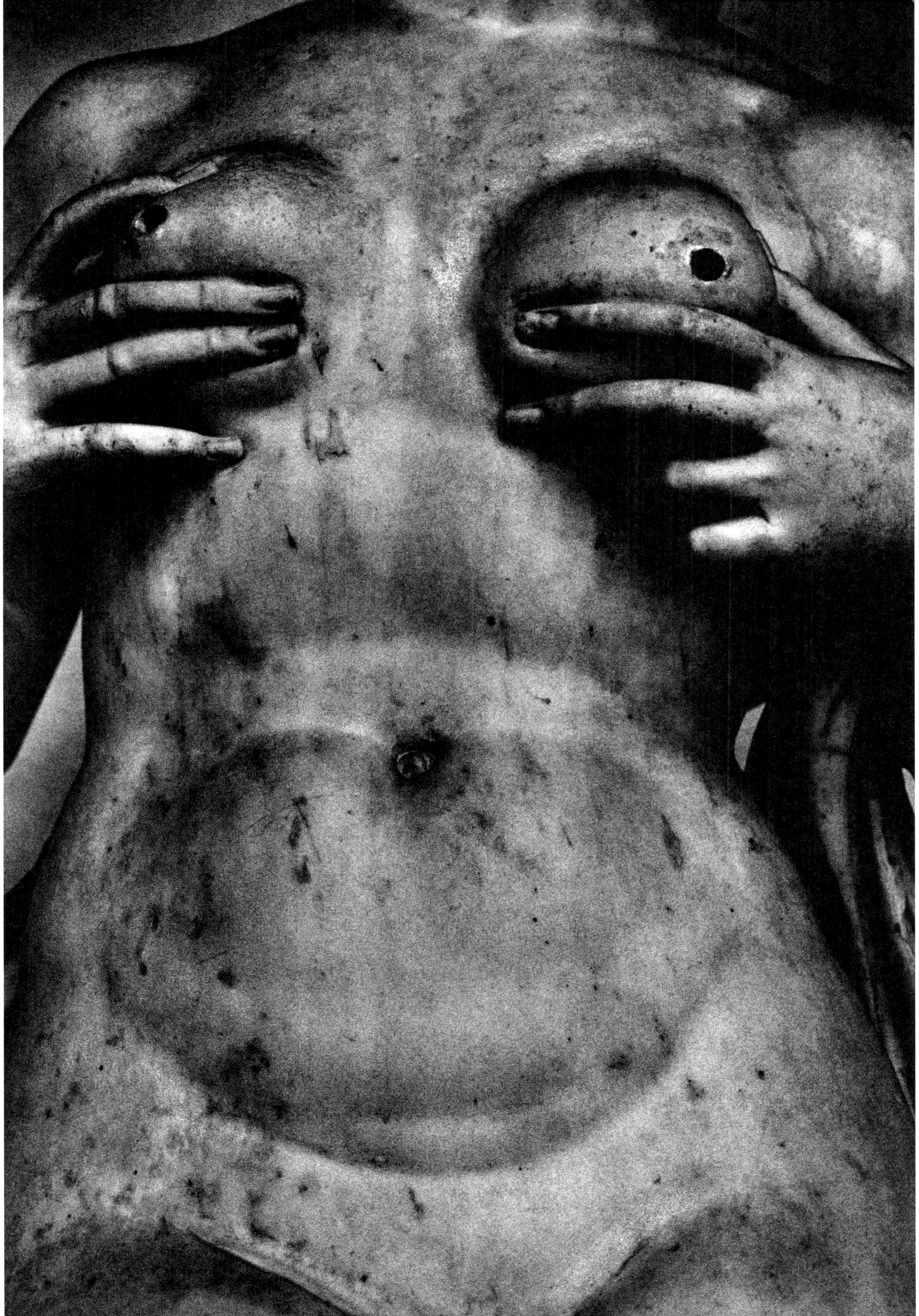

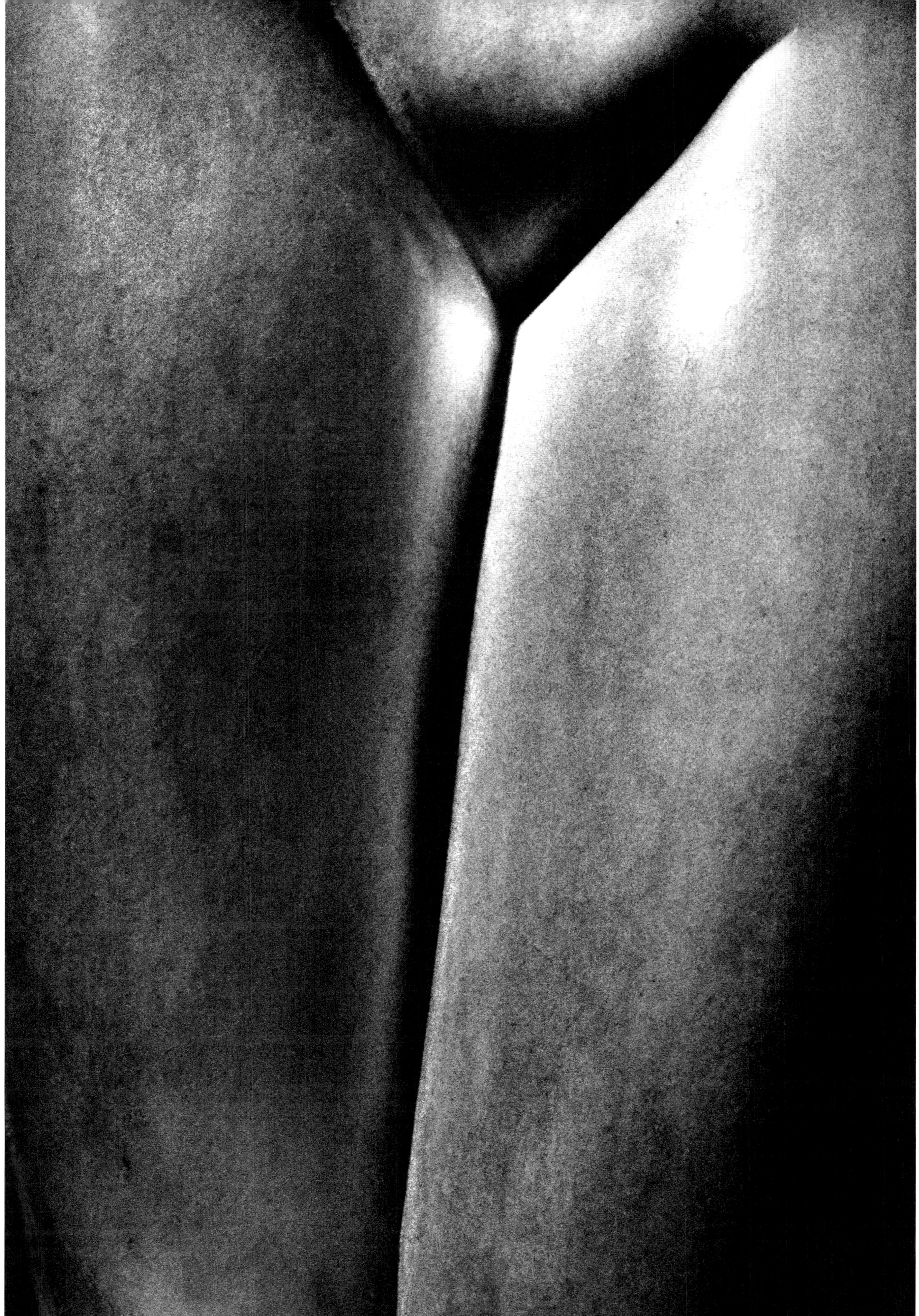

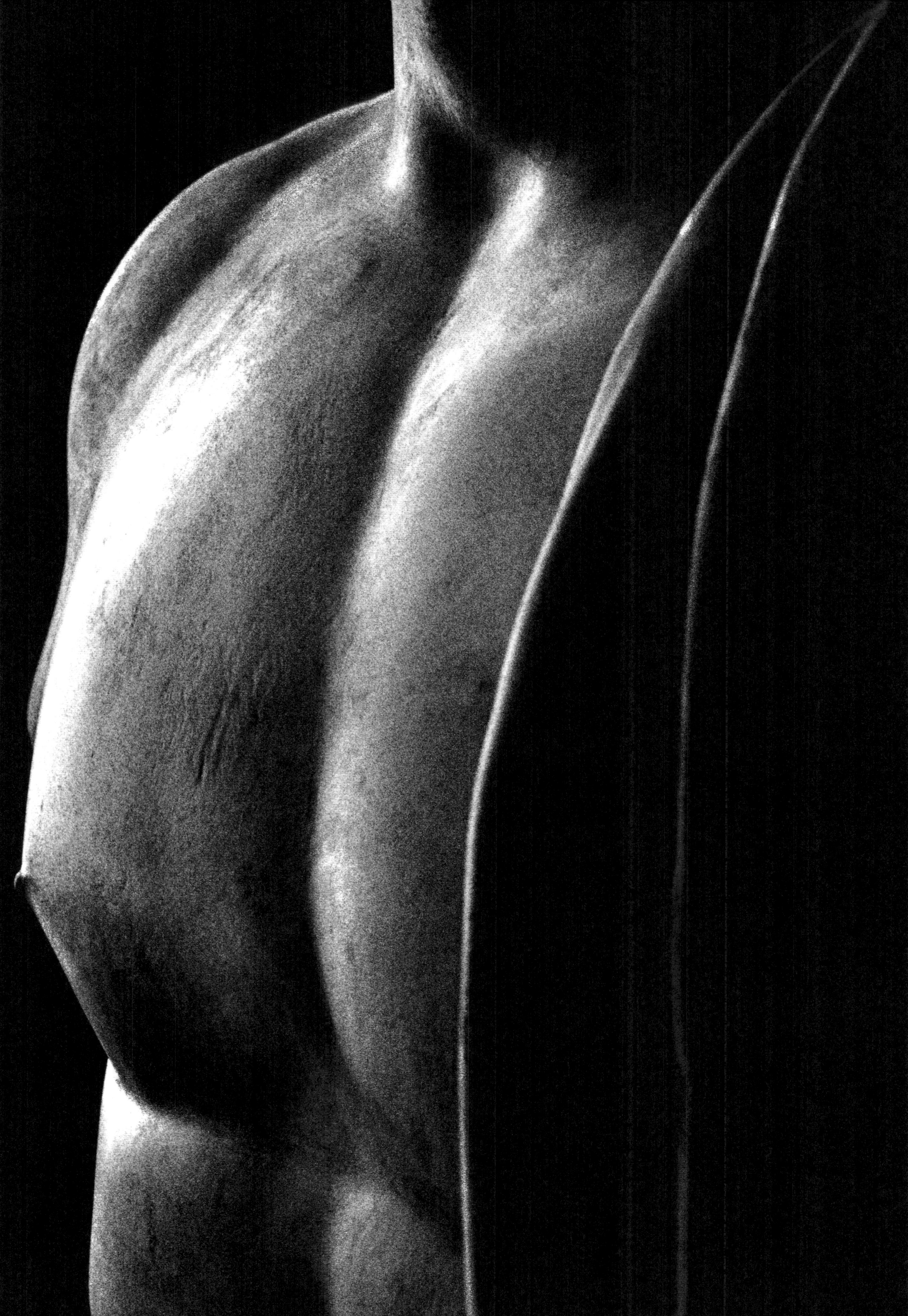

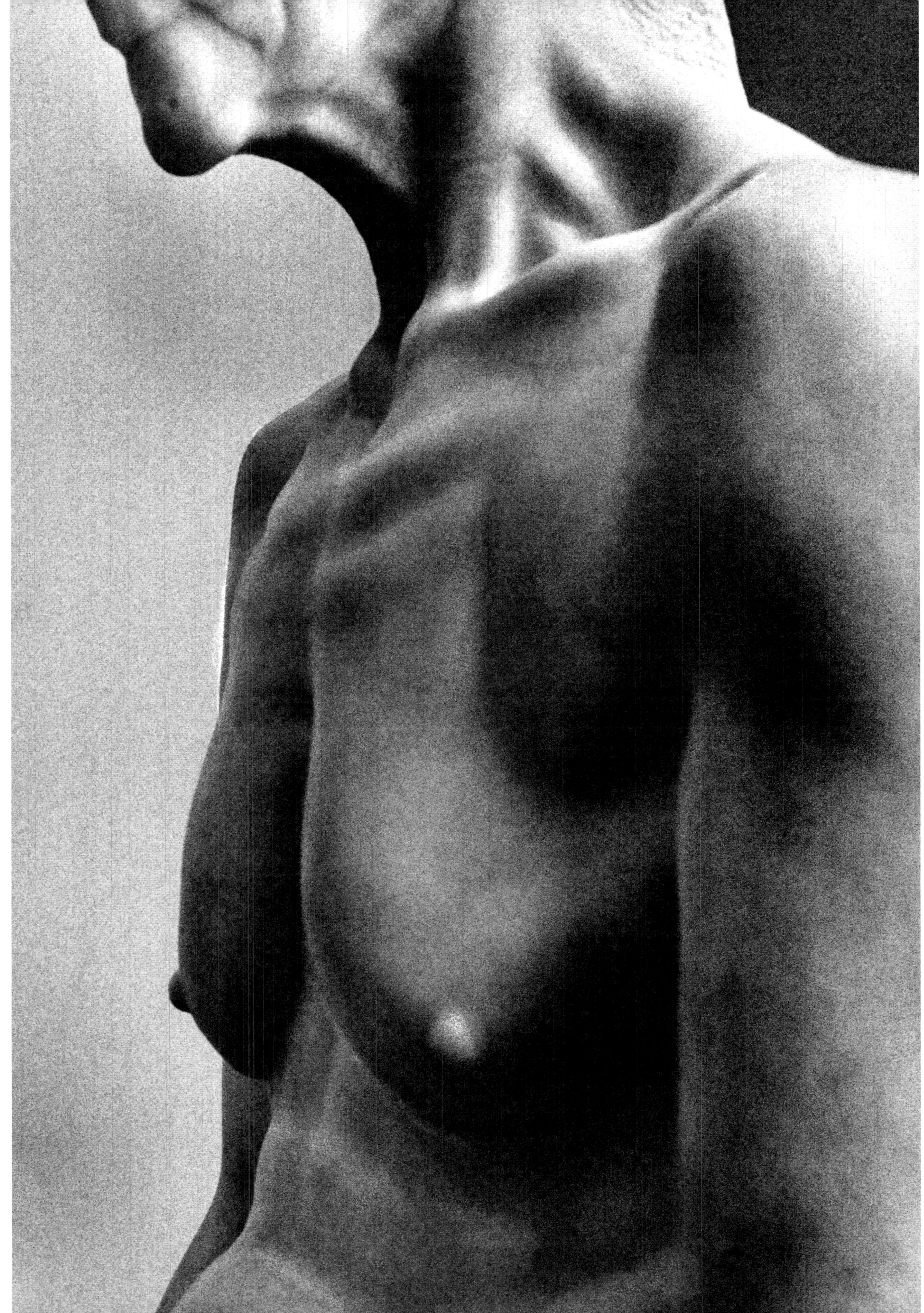

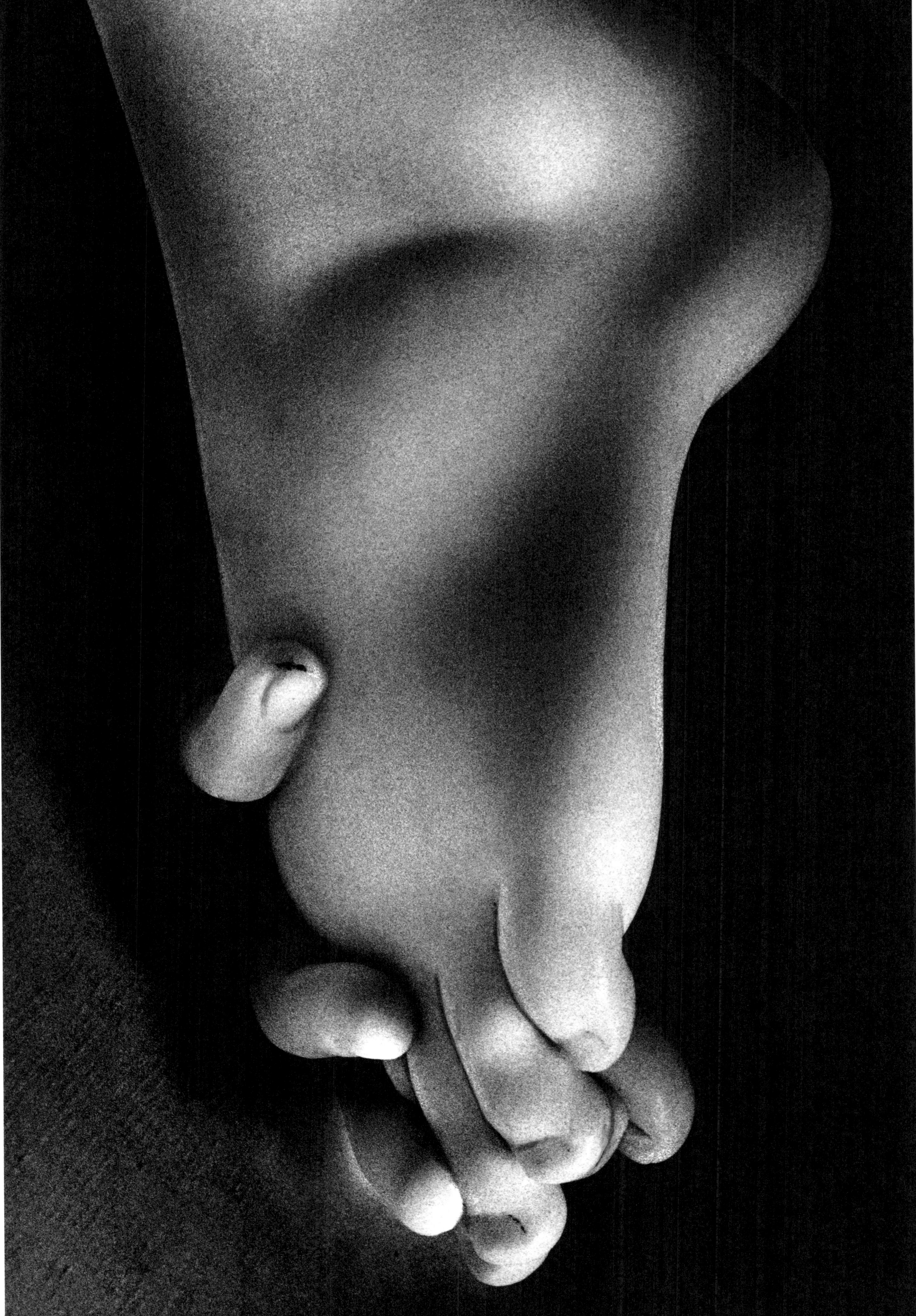

Living stone

Afterword by Phillippe Sollers

It is often said that photography gives the impression of life, but is in actual fact a kind of death. This is something that all great photographers know. Their art is close to black magic, and turning it into white magic requires total dedication. So Alejandra Figueroa, this tall dark-haired Mexican, playful, passionate and funny, very funny, set out to take anti-photos. From the very beginning she knew where to go: to sculpture, to marble. Rather than turning living things to stone, bringing stone alive. Rather than killing the moment, letting the centuries live. Rather than giving the illusion of a third dimension, releasing the fourth dimension of the relief, the modelling, the volume. These bodies, carefully worked by sculptors from all eras, are suddenly given a new and naked truth. The results are remarkable.

They are remarkable because they plunge us into the human body's movement throughout history. These are things we have never seen before: not just pieces of flesh, but pieces of music. Look at this white, this black, this grey white, this grey black, this white black, this black white, this black black, this white white. It is intoxicating and exhilarating. This is Beauty, as Baudelaire described it:

O mortals, I am lovely as a dream in stone;
My breast, where each may find his death by turns,
Inspires the poet with a love that burns
Forever, silent, like the earth alone.

Alejandra is the poet that Baudelaire speaks of. She takes up position, waits, watches, moves from shadow into light, steals, reveals, falls silent. She perceives the very essence of 'striking poses', which are themselves 'borrowed from the proudest monuments'. Beauty is eternal but elusive, hard to capture. It is a passion, a giant:

In times when fertile Nature filled the world
Each day with monstrous children, then would I
Have loved to live beside a giant girl,
Just as a cat by a queen's feet would lie.

What has been the goal of artists throughout history in their relationship with Beauty? Precisely this:

To wander her great contours as I please,
To climb the steep cliffs of her mighty knees...
To sleep at peace all shadowed by her breast.

It was in the mid-nineteenth century, in the graveyard of realism and naturalism, in a society of hypocritical modesty, that Baudelaire found himself moved by this Renaissance desire. Evidence of this lies in the poem from *The Flowers of Evil* called 'The Mask', an 'allegorical statue in the Renaissance taste', and dedicated to the sculptor Ernest Christophe (whose creations feature in Alejandra Figueroa's work).

Behold this Florentine marvel of graceful line;
This muscled form whose curves are filled
With Elegance and Strength, those twins divine
This miracle in flesh, this woman willed;
Divine robustness, lovely slenderness,
All made to crown the most sumptuous of beds
And charm a prince or pontiff's idleness.

Elegance and Strength – these are truly miracles in flesh.

The first image: is this the face of a drowned woman? Or is she only sleeping? Her eyes are dead, but her whole face is watching. She might even awaken, the photo seems to wish it. A calm block of stone, the relic of an unknown disaster, now discovered in serenity. What about the *Nymph With Scorpion*? Notice how the folds and hollows meet, how they interact with each other, the navel and breasts forming a secret temple. The next image seems almost a prayer, showing how an elbow may speak to a thigh or a calf, and a right hand to a left hand, and the fingers – ah, such fingers.

Next we see a trio, with folds of cloth, of knee, elbow and forearm. The right elbow is turned outwards, and rests on the knee of the crossed right leg; the left elbow is bent inwards, its hand thrusting back towards the stone body. Like the others, this image has incredible presence. It is immediately followed by a shadowy pubis, almost a shadowy mouth, a black hole that engulfs the camera. Then comes an ironic counterpoint: a small penis, a slender torso and slim legs. We have to wonder: could this be an hermaphrodite, are there breasts higher up? Alejandra is having fun in a serious way; she is teaching us the power of framing.

Then the head of a dying warrior takes us into the realm of tragedy: he seems a giant. From a small sex to a huge head. Next comes a trio of breast, navel and belly, followed by the towering architectural curves of a pair of buttocks. You have embarked on a journey of exploration, moving from the right way up to the wrong way around, from the detailed to the monumental. What you think you know about the human body is a lie; you are not even comfortable inside your own. Alejandra is not only a novelist and a poet but a moralist. Look at these modestly folded legs, or this head, a mask from the human comedy. Further still: could this be Aristaeus, the rustic god? Are we in Antiquity? No, in 1768, but no matter: it is the same story that is being told, the photograph is evidence enough. And as if you might have missed them, here are two enormous feet, stepping right out of the picture to tread on your toes. Then the next image: the rapt face of a baby.

A broken penis, legs like posts: what could this creature be? Tiny feet, or rather their soles. More curving hips, drapes of cloth, chests, breasts. Then lips, a chin, a neck, the lines of bitterness. The parts of the body continue to speak long after the whole: they become fragments of infinity, their seeming depersonalization makes them much more personal, part of an obstinate denial of lies, TV, advertising, control, marketing, public display, working out, beauty products, kitsch imagery. It is a grand refusal, haughty and aristocratic. A pair of legs seem to challenge you, a face appears somehow lit from within. More breasts and torsos, more buttocks and thighs, more bellies: you begin to understand that the journey never ends. An eye looks at a nipple; a nose and mouth interrupt a series of backs and torsos; a foot pokes out from the fray. Here is a shepherd holding an apple, the great prize for Beauty. The sculpture is by Nicolas François Gillet (1709–91). A male chest, an Adam's apple, a navel, a slight smile, the top of the head unseen: you begin to understand. Turn the page, and you are in 1561, with *Honour Triumphing Over Lies*: penis, groin, flaming curls of hair. Your attention is caught by a Greek Aphrodite; a hip, a calf, a hand, a foot. Death is not forgotten either: a funerary statue of Marguerite Valon (1674). How strange: she is only white stone from Plombières, yet she looks like an actress about to make her entrance on stage. Death too has its own life. Last of all, the splendid, triangular shape of a foot grasped by gentle fingers, the soft glow of porcelain.

Locations of sculptures featured in the photographs
Musée du Louvre, Paris; Musée d'Orsay, Paris;
Museo del Bargello, Florence; Hermitage Museum, St Petersburg;
Musei Capitolini, Rome; Museo Massimo, Rome;
Victoria & Albert Museum, London; Museo Nacional de México, Mexico City;
Friedrichwerdersche Kirche, Berlin; Pergamon-Museum, Berlin;
Musée des Beaux-Arts, Brussels; Cimitero Monumentale di Bologna, Bologna;
National Archaeological Museum, Athens; Russian Museum, St Petersburg;
Galleria Nazionale d'Arte Moderna, Rome; Academy of Fine Arts, St Petersburg.

Special thanks:
Guillermo, Laura Elena, Gabriela & Adriana Figueroa, Jean-Yves Brégand,
Benita Edzard and Gerhard Steidl.

Quentin Bajac, Leonello Brandolini, Geneviève Bresc-Bautier, Olivier Bourgoin,
Henri Coudoux, Robert Delpire, Agathe Gaillard, Didier Léger, John & Tana Morris,
Thomas Neurath, Víctor Flores Olea, Anne Pagiot, Edouard Papet, Gaëlle Quentin,
Georges-Elia Sarfati, Philippe Sollers and Patrick Toussant.

Claudia Barron, Catherine Bélanger, Cecilia Bilesio, Joel Brard,
Krystel Boula, Patricia Cao-Romero, Leticia Clouthier, Leon Constantiner,
Paula Cussi, Jacques-Olivier David, Monica Delgado, Guadalupe Duran,
François Eschapasse, Miguel & Mercedes Fernández Félix, Jacklin Hameur,
Alix de Foras, Agnès de Gouvion Saint-Cyr, Claude Helft, Adela & Claude Heller,
Pascal Hoel, Sylvie & Olivier Lebois, Carmen & Alexander Mariscal,
Juan Martínez, Valerie Meyer, Igor Mitorai, Christophe Monin,
Jean-Luc Monterosso, Elisabeth Nora, Alexander Oppersdorff,
Brigitte Ollier, Sandro Parmigiani, Hélène Pinet, Françoise Rousset,
Rafael & Ana Laura Samano, Claudia & Carlos Salcido, Dimitri Salomon,
Anne Sanciaud, Philippe Tarabella, Angela Tromellini, Graciela de la Torre,
Jorge Volpi, Paul Williamson, Kasia Wyderko, Oda Zborowski,
Julián & Nathalie Zugazagoitia, Laboratoire Imaginoir
and all staff at Steidl Publishers.

I am very grateful to all of the sculptors who rest in peace,
may they not turn in their graves. A. F.

First published in the United Kingdom in 2003 by
Thames & Hudson Ltd, 181A High Holborn, London WC1V 7QX

www.thamesandhudson.com

British Library Cataloguing-in-Publication Data
A catalogue record for this book is available from the British Library

ISBN 0-500-54281-3

Printed and bound in Germany by Steidl, Göttingen